Pablo Antoni)

THE BIRTH OF THE SUN

Translated by Steven F. White

A Series of Translations of
Poetries

SPONSORED BY

THE WITTER BYNNER FOUNDATION FOR POETRY, INC.

and

UNICORN FOUNDATION
FOR THE ADVANCEMENT OF MODERN POETRY

John Balaban & Teo Savory, *Editors of the Series*

VOLUME I

Poets of Bulgaria

Edited by William Meredith

VOLUME II

Woman on the Front Lines

Belkis Cuza Malé

VOLUME III

The Birth of the Sun

Pablo Antonio Cuadra

The Birth of the Sun

PABLO ANTONIO CUADRA

Selected Poems 1935-1985

Translated by
Steven F. White

1988
Greensboro
Unicorn Press, Inc.

Some of the translations previously appeared in *New Directions Annual 46*, *Northwest Review*, and *The American Voice*, and are reprinted here with the permission of the editors.

The reproductions of the woodblocks in *The Jaguar and the Moon*, one of which appears on the cover of this book, are by Pablo Antonio Cuadra. The photograph of the author was taken by Steven F. White in Managua, Nicaragua. All rights reserved by Unicorn Press.

Assistance in publication was received from The Witter Bynner Foundation for Poetry, the North Carolina Arts Council, and the National Endowment for the Arts, a Federal Agency in Washington, D.C.

Teo Savory, editor-in-chief of Unicorn Press, wishes to thank Anita Richardson of Universal Printing, Greensboro, for typesetting this book (in 11 pt Baskerville and Garamond High Density), and McNaughton & Gunn, Ann Arbor, for printing it (on 60# Glatfelter); *designed by Alan Brilliant*. Sarah Lindsay copy-edited and proof-read this book, which was clothbound by Leigh Carter.

Library of Congress Cataloguing-in-Publication Data

Cuadra, Pablo Antonio, 1912-
   The birth of the sun.
   (A Series of translations of poetries; v.3)
   English and Spanish.
   Bibliography: p.
   1. Cuadra, Pablo Antonio, 1912-   —Translations, English.   I. White,
   Steven F., 1955-   II. Title.   III. Series.
   PQ7519.C8A28   1988   861   86-25065
   ISBN 0-87775-204-4
   ISBN 0-87775-205-2 (pbk.)

Unicorn Press Inc./P.O. Box 3307/Greensboro, NC 27402

Table of Contents

IV.   SONGS OF CIFAR

Introduction to the Poetry
of Pablo Antonio Cuadra

By Jorge Eduardo Arellano

At the beginning of 1934, Pablo Antonio Cuadra (born in Managua, Nicaragua, on November 4, 1912) took his first trip abroad. He went as the secretary of his father, the famous speaker and intellectual Carlos Cuadra Pasos (1879-1964), who was one of the Nicaraguan delegates to the Panamerican Conference in Montevideo, Uruguay. Pablo Antonio Cuadra took advantage of these circumstances to become personally acquainted with the people involved in the literary and political movements in several South American countries. In Buenos Aires, in addition to meeting Federico García Lorca, he became involved with *Renovación*. This literary group had doctrines and ideals similar to those of the young writers in Nicaragua who were associated with the movement known as the *Vanguardia*. The writers of the *Vanguardia* first gathered in Granada, Nicaragua, from 1927 to 1930 and came into their own as writers from 1931 to 1933.

Oswaldo Horacio Dondo, one of Cuadra's friends at that time, remembers Cuadra "reading. . . a book by Ramiro de Maeztú, *Defensa de la Hispanidad*. He spoke of Garcilaso, Fray Luis de León, Santa Teresa, Menéndez Pelayo, Donoso Cortés, Rubén Darío and Leopoldo Lugones. Cuadra's words were those of a patient poet and a patient Catholic: *Build it! Little by little. With help from everyone. Put things in order, piece by piece.*" Ever since, this has been Cuadra's conviction, something that has enabled him to channel his work into three simultaneous currents: a poetry of human solidarity that bears witness to love and faith in Christ as forces of salvation; a poetry of civility and dignity; and a poetry of culture that is a search for the identity, voice and spirit of his people. But these currents can also be recognized in the poet's other great allegiance: Cuadra makes his vital Nicaraguan experience universal.

This process began with *Canciones de pájaro y señora* (1929-1931), a collection of poems which, although lacking maturity, nevertheless explains Cuadra's evolution as the author of *Poemas nicaragüenses* (1930-1933). While the latter is the most representative work of his generation in the 1930s, the former is indistinguishable from the writings of the other members of his group who aspired to the same ideals as Cuadra. These writers were all engaged in a creative search for the traditional forms of anonymous poetry and for certain Nicaraguan motifs.

Cuadra saw in folklore a source that would enable him to create a vernacular poetry. For this reason, he took as inspiration the popular forms of the *romance*, the *corrido*, songs and children's games—modes of expression that were still alive in the rural parts of Nicaragua. In order to achieve a language that was colloquial as well as stylized and graceful, Cuadra modified the traditional Hispanic *zejel* of Arabic origin and used meters and repeating rhymes in his poetry associated with songs played on guitar. A good example of this kind of writing is the four-line poem "Intervention" in which the poet says to a Yankee marine occupying Nicaragua *"go jón"* and to the cute gringa *"very güel."* In fact, Cuadra's early poetry tends to derive Nicaraguan identity from an Hispanic legacy and a rejection of the United States intervention in Nicaragua.

If, in *Canciones de pájaro y señora*, Cuadra assimilates the vernacular, in *Poemas nicaragüenses* (his second book, chrono-logically speaking) he establishes a national poetry in Central America. *Poemas nicaragüenses* is a book in which Cuadra sings his "third class country." He captures the landscape, geography and abundant natural world of Nicaragua and, in the face of foreign intervention, Cuadra exalts a national identity.

Poemas nicaragüenses, Cuadra's first book in print, was brought out by Nascimento publishers in Santiago, Chile, in 1934. About the circumstances surrounding its appearance, Cuadra has said, "Friends of mine in Chile who were poets urged me to publish the manuscript I had with me right away so that I could read my poems during my first journey through South America. When they were published, however, I realized that the poems were unfinished and I began to correct them, to recreate them in an intense and continuous labor during 1935." In spite of the rough, unshaped poems contained in the first edition of *Poemas nicaragüenses*, one can distinguish two of the poet's future orientations: the assimilation of the cosmic spirit of the earth and a deep-rooted sense of Catholicism. Both are main-tained formally when the poet reworks his poetry in 1935 and gives it an architectonic sense. This applies not only to *Poemas nica-ragüenses*, but also to another collection of poems written during Cuadra's travels through South America—a dozen poems called *Cuaderno del Sur* that Cuadra did not publish until 1982.

Poemas nicaragüenses and *Cuaderno del Sur* are books of discovery by means of traveling: toward the interior of the poet's country in the first book, and outside it (South America) in the second. In both, one senses the eye of the traveler that, in terms of literature, comes from the reading of French poets such as Blaise Cendrars, Valery Larbaud, Paul Morand and, above all, Jules Supervielle. Supervielle is the source of Cuadra's dazzling penetration of every corner of Nicaragua, beginning with the heroic region in the north known as the Segovias in his "Poem of the Foreigners' Moment in Our Jungle":

> In the heart of our mountains, where the old jungle
> devours roads the way the *guás* eats snakes,
> where Nicaragua raises its flag of blazing rivers among torrential
>   drums. . .
> There, long before my song,
> even before I existed, I invent the stone called flint
> and I ignite the sordid green of *heliconias*,
> the mangroves' boiling silence,
> and I set fire to the orchid in the boa constrictor's night.

In this poem, Nature, reduced to the world's totality, devours the invaders—the 500 North Americans who burn the farms of the indigenous people and whose "white bones [are] delicately polished by the ants."

Like a native Adam, the poet names the things of the world around him—innumerable quantities of natural and human elements that belong to an agricultural tradition with colonial roots. Cuadra becomes acquainted with all this as the son of someone who owns a ranch, but transcends it through the word and his own imagination. In other words, Cuadra incorporates an historical and geographic legacy and then surpasses it by means of a powerful perception of the world.

From the perspective of the rural, land-owning class inherited from his ancestors, Cuadra builds a personal republic inhabited by dignified peasants: "Not all the men among my people/cluster together like sheep. . ./Not all of them offer their faces to the whip of "no,"/or ask for charity./I have seen dignity" ("Third Class Country"). Cuadra travels his country on horseback, incorporating a free and primitive rhythm in the majority of his overflowing poems. "It was Supervielle," wrote Cuadra in 1980, "who taught me how to make poetry on horseback." Cuadra does not remain solely in the region of Nicaragua called Chontales. He goes to Chinandega, passing through Masaya; he lives in Rivas and in his Granada that he carries with him always. The beautiful names of the remote areas he visits are placed at the end of his *Nicaraguan Poems:* Márgenes del Tepenaguasapa, Gran Llano de Apompúa, Serranías del Este,

Hacienda "Animas," Paso de Lajas, Alamicamba, Posoltega, San Ubaldo, El Menco, Olama, Mombacho, Santa Elisa, etc.

Cuadra's poetic discovery of the country is a response to the intervention (both armed and cultural) of the United States in Nicaragua from 1926 to 1932. In this sense, guided by a national identity derived from his Hispanic heritage, Cuadra rejects the intervention and allies himself with the nationalistic resistance of General Augusto C. Sandino. Cuadra admires and praises Sandino in one of his poems ("Son-sonete") from the 1934 Nascimento edition which the poet reworks, changing the title to "The Airplane's Old Engine" in 1935. This poem tells of a foreign pilot shot down by the Sandinistas, a feat unknown to the local residents in the city. The poem ends:

> Only you, guerrilla, with your restless loyalty to native skies,
> standing guard since dawn in the high branches of the ocote tree,
> will preserve this lost history in song.

As many critics have recognized and celebrated, Cuadra affirms a nationality as a defensive strategy. Nicaragua's current ambassador to the United States, Carlos Tunnerman Bernheim, once wrote: "During the years of North American occupation, Nicaragua produced two great testimonies of nationalism: Sandino in the mountains and Pablo Antonio Cuadra in his *Poemas nicaragüenses.*" Cuadra also *establishes* his country by taking stock of it in minute detail, ordering its most intimate things and places, evaluating popular traditions, creating portraits of millenary figures, and telling tales (from the omnipresent vegetation) of frustrated loves. It is from Cuadra's promised land, then, that the poet formulates an entire program: "I must make something from the mud of history,/dig down in the swamp and unearth the moons/of my forefathers" ("Poem of the Foreigners' Moment in Our Jungle").

Cuadra continues pursuing the task of making his personal aspirations universal in his next book, *Canto temporal*, published in 1943. The impact of World War II produced a spiritual crisis in the poet that was also linked to the failure of the literary/political project undertaken by the poets of the Nicaraguan Vanguard. The *vanguardistas* had allied themselves with the Somoza dictatorship, hoping for a patriarchal, corporativist (Mussolini-style) political restoration inspired by Christian ideals. It was this desire for "an order like a gigantic column" (Canto III) that leads the poet to an intense searching of his interior world that includes the innocence he experienced as a child, the dissatisfaction with human love, and the recognition of the peasant as a human model in direct contact with the elements. The poet discovers that what is universal can only be found fully in the truth of Christ.

Cuadra's next book, *Libro de horas*, written in Mexico, Spain and Nicaragua from 1946 to 1954, has a rich Biblical tone. This is a work in which Cuadra attempts to fuse the spirit and form of medieval books with the poetry and songs of the pre-Columbian Indian codices. Cuadra explains it as "that which links time and nature with Christian mysteries." The poems in *Libro de horas* are immersed in a spirit of Christian jubilation and solidarity. In "National Anthem (At Daybreak)," the poet creates his country in an intimate dialogue with the land and his people whom he addresses by name:

You, José Muñoz, carpenter by trade, maker of my table,
take this star. Go out and guide its hour. Fix it!
And you, Martín Zepeda, already on the road, gather
these birds. Give them song or tell them
what you know about bread and guitars.
And you, Pedro Canisal, cowhand, young and rustic:
put your saddle on the horizon, climb the heights
of the night and tame it!

Everyone is convoked by the poet and his compassion for humanity in order to build a new dawn.

At the age of 45, Cuadra undertook a remarkable change in his lyric poetry—the discovery of Myth. Purifying himself to the maximum degree, Cuadra followed the advice of Plato: "A poet, in order to truly be a poet, should not compose speeches in verse, but invent myths." In this way, to enrich his poetry, Cuadra besieged the mythology of Central America—the zone to which the principal pre-Hispanic cultures of his country belonged. These sources qualitatively change Cuadra's poetry beginning with his book *El Jaguar y la luna* (1959).

Inspired by the striking ceramics of Nicaraguan indigenous cultures, these poems assimilate the tradition of Nahuatl poetry and achieve an agile conciseness either to draw excellent, imperishable miniatures or to obtain testimonies of profound significance. Thomas Merton wrote the following about *El Jaguar y la luna*, a book he translated: "Certain aspects of his verse are social and political. He cannot do otherwise than attempt. . . to clarify contemporary aspirations in the language of ancient myth."

Cuadra completes the rescue of the marginal figures of history in *Cantos de Cifar y de la mar dulce* (1971), adding a Homeric contribution to his work that had been essentially Virgilian. It has a narrative strength and resembles a novel concentrated in verse. Cuadra assimilates the ancestral myths of Nicaragua and· the everyday life of the people who live on the shores of Nicaragua's Great Lake. The poet achieves this by means of a balanced presentation of new forms and rhythms. The songs of *Cantos de Cifar* have popular roots but are not tied completely to tradition. At the same time, Cuadra's humble epic is permeated by allusions to the classics.

The process of making what is Nicaraguan universal continues in *Esos rostros que asoman en la multitud* (1976), a book guided by a deep sense of Christian compassion that confronts the horror of history. The faces in the crowd in this book are portraits of dozens of anonymous Nicaraguans searching for a country where they can live in freedom.

Siete árboles contra el atardecer (1980), in addition to summarizing (both technically and conceptually) Cuadra's entire expressive trajectory, is a book that unites the poet's ethical and humanistic thought. This is because the seven trees *(Siete árboles)*, sustained by the weight of the years, take a stand against the dying light *(contra el atardecer)* and signify the struggle and victory of humanity. And this defense of human values on the part of the poet goes beyond any ideological roots.

Cuadra's poem "September: The Shark," which belongs to the forthcoming book *Tun—la ronda del año—(poemas para un calendario)*, is the poet's final, total vision. Cuadra's stance against "evil" is based on his view of the history of Nicaragua, a country he feels has been threatened and destroyed by terrifying forces from the different epochs of history: the wars between the indigenous tribes, the Spaniards from the time of Columbus, the pirates of the seventeenth century, William Walker, the capitalists from the United States, and, now, Fidel Castro.

Cuadra's poetry is a significant example of a phenomenon characteristic of Nicaraguan poetry: the transcending of ideology. If it is true that the artist has been conditioned historically and socially, and that his ideological positions play a certain role in terms of artistic creation, this does not imply the need for the poet to reduce his work to his own ideological ingredients. This is especially true of Cuadra, whose search for the universal enables him to go beyond the social/historical humus that gave birth to his poetry and thereby bridge the gap between people of different social classes. At the same time, as a national poet who has captured the essence of his country, Cuadra has written poetry that has become synonymous with Nicaragua.

I

ANTHEMS

NONANTZIN

(Traducción libre de Netzahualcoyotl)

Amada, si yo muriera
entiérrame en la cocina
bajo el fogón.

Al palmotear la tortilla
me llamará a su manera
tu corazón.

Más si alguien, amor, se empeña
en conocer tu pesar
dile que es verde la leña
y hace llorar.

NONANTZIN

(Imitation of a poem by Netzahualcoyotl)

My love, if I die,
bury me beneath the hearth
where you prepare meals.

As your hands shape the tortilla,
your heart will call me
the way it used to.

But if anyone, my love, keeps asking
about your sorrow,
tell them the wood is green
and makes you weep.

PATRIA DE TERCERA

Viajando en tercera he visto
un rostro.
No todos los hombres de mi pueblo
óvidos, claudican.
He visto un rostro.
Ni todos doblan su papel en barquichuelos
para charco. Viajando he visto
el rostro de un huertero.
Ni todos ofrecen su faz al látigo del "no"
ni piden.
La dignidad he visto.
Porque no sólo fabricamos huérfanos,
o bien, inadvertidos,
criamos cuervos.
He visto un rostro austero. Serenidad
o sol sobre su frente
como un título (ardiente y singular).
Nosotros ¡ah! rebeldes
al hormiguero
si algún día damos
la cara al mundo:
con los rasgos usuales de la Patria
¡un rostro enseñaremos!

THIRD CLASS COUNTRY

Travelling in third class, I have seen
a face.
Not all the men among my people
cluster together like sheep.
I have seen a face.
Not all of them fold paper boats
to sail puddles. Travelling, I have seen
the face of a farmer.
Not all of them offer their faces to the whip of "no,"
or ask for charity.
I have seen dignity.
Because we do not simply manufacture orphans,
or, inadvertently,
raise crows as children.
I have seen an austere face. Peace
or sunlight on the forehead
like some kind of fiery, unique credentials.
If only we, the rebels
against the anthill, marked by the usual
traits of our country, could show
our face to the world!

POR LOS CAMINOS VAN LOS CAMPESINOS. . .

De dos en dos,
de diez en diez,
de cien en cien,
de mil en mil,
descalzos van los campesinos
con la chamarra y el fusil.

De dos en dos los hijos han partido,
de cien en cien las madres han llorado,
de mil en mil los hombres han caído,
y hecho polvo ha quedado
su sueño en la chamarra, su vida en el fusil.

El rancho abandonado,
la milpa sola, el frijolar quemado.
El pájaro volando
sobre la espiga muda
y el corazón llorando
su lágrima desnuda.

De dos en dos,
de diez en diez,
de cien en cien,
de mil en mil,
descalzos van los campesinos
con la chamarra y el fusil.

THE CAMPESINOS GO DOWN THE ROADS

Two by two,
ten by ten,
by hundreds
and thousands,
the *campesinos* go barefoot
with their bedrolls and their rifles.

Two by two the sons have left,
hundreds of mothers have cried,
thousands of men have fallen
and turned to dust forever
dreaming on their bedrolls
about the life that was their rifle.

The abandoned ranch,
the lonely fields of corn,
the fields of beans destroyed by fire.
The birds flying over mute stalks
and the heart crying
its naked tears.

Two by two,
ten by ten,
by hundreds and thousands
the *campesinos* are leaving
barefoot with their bedrolls and their rifles.

De dos en dos,
de diez en diez,
de cien en cien,
de mil en mil,
¡por los caminos van los campesinos
a la guerra civil!

Two by two,
ten by ten,
by hundreds
and thousands
the *campesinos* go down the roads
to fight the civil war!

EL VIEJO MOTOR DE AEROPLANO

En el Valle de "Ciudad Antigua"
a doce leguas cansadas de la ciudad de Nueva Segovia
los campesinos vendieron un viejo motor de aeroplano.

Era una noche de mil novecientos veinticinco
ceñida de jazmines como las doncellas que mueren sin amante.

La avioneta equipada con ametralladoras y raros telescopios
cubrió de sangre las húmedas espadas del trigal
y el más viejo aviador de la armada
abandonó sus cruces de plata por una muerte trágica y violenta.

Nadie reconoció en las palpitaciones noticiosas de los diarios
aquella hermosa cerviz californiana
que tuvo la osadía de batirse cuerpo a cuerpo con las nubes de Hawai.
La ciudad hormigueante, a solicitud de los grandes avisos de color,
penetraba con vagos anhelos deportivos en los cinemas y los bares
mientras a la luz terrosa de los barrios los niños con papeles
reproducían aviones y volvían a la muerte
asesinando las aves forasteras.

Las esquivas coloraciones del inmenso valle anaranjado y violeta
tomaban en la soledad asfixiante de las fotografías
el extraño matiz de los sueños oprimidos por el miedo.
—Ahí estaba postrado el gran esqueleto del pájaro
y la gorra destrozada con las altas insignias militares—.

THE AIRPLANE'S OLD ENGINE

In the valley of "Ciudad Antigua,"
which is twelve tiring leagues from the city of Nueva Segovia,
the campesinos sold an airplane's old engine.

It was 1925, on a night covered with jasmine blossoms
like young girls who die without knowing love.

The airplane, equipped with machine-guns and strange telescopic sights,
covered the swords of the wheatfield with blood
and the squadron's oldest pilot
gave up his silver medals for a tragic and violent death.

In the newspapers' pulse of events, nobody
recognized the profile of the Californian
who once dared to fight Hawaiian clouds in direct combat.
The teeming city's walls were plastered with colorful signs
and in the cinemas and bars the talk was of sports.
But in the earthen light of the poor barrios,
children made paper airplanes and confronted death
by killing the foreign birds.

In the suffocating loneliness of a photograph,
the elusive coloring of the immense orange and violet valley
took on the strange tint of dreams oppressed by fear:
there was the great skeleton of the bird stretched out
and the shredded flight cap with high-ranking military insignia.

Se ignoraba el motivo.
Los más antiguos científicos indagaron las capas atmosféricas
donde antes solamente vagaban
las ansiosas pupilas de los sembradores que interrogan al sol
y los pájaros de tendencias musicales.

Luego durmieron los ricos comerciantes y las jóvenes hermosas.
Una dama de negro recibía esquelas enlutadas
y se preparaban los alcaldes para nuevas agitaciones.

Sólo tú —guerrillero— con tu inquieta lealtad a los aires nativos
centinela desde el alba en las altas vigilias del ocote
guardarás para el canto esta historia perdida.

No one knows how it happened.
The oldest scientists investigated the atmospheric layers
where, before, there was only the sun
questioned by the eyes of peasant farmers
and the flight of singing birds.

Then the rich merchants and the beautiful young women went to sleep.
A woman dressed in mourning received the cards outlined in black
and mayors braced themselves for more unrest.

Only you, guerrilla, with your restless loyalty to native skies,
standing guard since dawn in the high branches of the ocote tree,
will preserve this lost history in song.

POEMA DEL MOMENTO EXTRANJERO EN LA SELVA

(A varias voces.)

En el corazón de nuestras montañas donde la vieja selva
devora los caminos como el guás las serpientes
donde Nicaragua levanta su bandera de ríos flameando entre tambores
[torrenciales
allí, anterior a mi canto
anterior a mí mismo invento el pedernal
y alumbro el verde sórdido de las heliconias,
el hirviente silencio de los manglares
y enciendo la orquídea en la noche de la toboba.
Llamo. Grito. ¡Estrella, ¿quién ha abierto las puertas de la noche?
Tengo que hacer algo con el lodo de la historia,
cavar en el pantano y desenterrar la luna
de mis padres. ¡Oh! ¡Desata
tu oscura cólera víbora magnética,
afila tus obsidianas tigre negro, clava
tu fosforescente ojo ¡allí!
En la médula del bosque
500 norteamericanos!

Vienen marchando.
Cantan entre sotocaballos y ñámbaros
Cantan al paso y caen
desde las altas copas las últimas lunas nicaragüenses.

(Rojas lapas hablan lenguas locas.)
En el corazón de nuestras montañas 500 marinos entran con ametralladora
Oigo voces.

POEM OF THE FOREIGNERS' MOMENT IN OUR JUNGLE

(for several voices)

In the heart of our mountains, where the old jungle
devours roads the way the *guás* eats snakes,
where Nicaragua raises its flag of blazing rivers among torrential drums. . .
There, long before my song,
even before I existed, I invent the stone called flint
and I ignite the sordid green of *heliconias*,
the mangroves' boiling silence,
and I set fire to the orchid in the boa constrictor's night.
I cry out. Scream. Star! Who just opened the night's doors?
I must make something from the mud of history,
dig down in the swamp and unearth the moons
of my forefathers. Oh, unleash
your dark rage, magnetic snake,
sharpen your obsidian claws, black tiger, stare
with your phosphorescent eyes, there!
      In the heart of the jungle,
      500 North Americans!

They're marching,
singing among the *sotocaballos* and the *ñámbaros*,
singing to the rhythm of their marching feet.
And Nicaragua's last moons plummet from treetops.

(Red macaws chatter in crazy tongues.)
In the heart of our mountains, 500 Marines with machine-guns make their way.
I hear voices.

Túngala del sapo
Túngala
Túngala
Andrés Regules —"tu escopeta era prohibida"—
Ahora cuelgas del manglar.
Orlando Temolián
Fermín Maguel (túngala, túngala).
Acripena, su esposa (todos mískitos)
más altas que las palmeras las llamas del caserío.

Quinientos norteamericanos hacen la guerra.

Los árboles tienen su fruto en secreto.
Oigo voces

Túngala
Túngala
Los niños en los pipantes
navegan huérfanos.

Pero hemos dicho que la selva es un viejo animal sobre la tumba de
[nuestros muertos
Hemos dicho que en el árbol de la noche el silencio empolla gavilanes
[furiosos.
Oigo voces.
Túngala, grita el sapo
Túngala, clama el sapo-buey
Top, top, top, atestigua la iniquidad
el gran pájaro del sotocaballo.
Y vemos llegar al Pálido,
al Ojeroso-del-Alba con sus nubes de mosquitos zumbando y saliendo de
[las cuencas de su calavera
Y oímos sonar sus diminutos clarines
de pantano en pantano.

The bullfrog's *Túngula*
Túngula
Túngula
Andrés Regules, "Your shotgun is against the law."
Now you hang from the branch of a mangrove tree.
Orlando Temolián.
Fermín Maguel *(túngula, túngula)*,
Acripena, his wife (all Mískito Indians).
The flames of the burning village leap higher than palm trees.

Five hundred North Americans making war.

The trees secretly bear their fruit.
I hear voices.
       Túngula
       Túngula
Those children steering dugouts
are orphans.

But we've said that the jungle is an old animal stretched across the tomb of all
    our dead.
We've said that in the tree of night fierce hawks hatch from silence.

I hear voices.
Túngula, cries the toad.
Túngula, protests the bullfrog.
Top, top, top. The great *sotocaballo*
bird bears witness to the iniquity.
Here come the palefaces,
dark rings under their eyes at dawn, clouds of mosquitoes
buzzing and entering any openings in their skulls.
And in the distance we hear their bugles call
from swamp to swamp.

¡Ah, vosotras!, neblinas húmedas
—grita—. ¡Ah!, nubes húmedas
nubes de inextinguible estridencia
Finas espadas de la fiebre
Anófeles
ínfimas águilas del pequeño escudo pisoteado
"e plúribus unum"
¡Ah!
. . .presenciamos
el retiro precipitado de 500 norteamericanos
pálidamente derrotados
quemadas las sangres por la última llama del rancho de Acripena,
temblando el frío de la muerte de Andrés Regules,
el frío de la muerte de Orlando Temolián,
de Fermín Maguel (todos mískitos)
500 norteamericanos van huyendo,
maláricos
rastros perdidos de pantano en pantano
delirantes
Túngala
Túngala
El gran sapo salta, compadre,
La lluvia llama otra vez.
Oigo voces: las arañas azules
tejen una nueva bandera virgen.
Anterior a mi canto
anterior a mí mismo,
en el corazón de nuestras montañas
donde invento el pedernal y alumbro
bajo el verde sórdido de las heliconias
bajo el hirviente silencio de los manglares
sus blancos huesos delicadamente pulidos por las hormigas.

"Ah!" shout the palefaces. Damp fog.

"Ah!" Damp clouds,

implacably harsh clouds,

slender swords of fever.

Anopheles.

Vulgar eagles from their tiny, trampled coins

e pluribus unum

"Ah!"

We witness

the frenzied retreat of 500 North Americans,

defeated and pale,

their blood burned by the last flames of Acripena's farm,

trembling with the cold of Andrés Regules's death,

the cold of Orlando Temolián's death,

Fermín Maguel's (all Mískito Indians).

500 fleeing North Americans,

with malaria,

their footprints lost from swamp to swamp,

delirious,

Túngula

Túngula.

The great frog leaps, my friend.

The rain calls once again.

I hear voices: the blue spiders

weave a new virgin flag.

Before my song,

even before I existed,

in the heart of our mountains,

beneath the sordid green of *heliconias,*

beneath the mangroves' boiling silence,

I invent the stone called flint

and I ignite their white bones delicately polished by the ants.

INAUGURACION DE LOS ANDES POR DIOS

Una lágrima de cocodrilo puede ser el comienzo del Nilo.
En mi tierra un diocesillo llamado Cocijo
allí donde orina hace nacer un río.
Un copo de nieve —como una cana al aire— del Chimborazo
puede haber caído de las sienes de Dios
                              que mueve
sus manos bíblicas de alfarero y pule las cumbres.
                    El indio invoca a Wirakocha
y un viejo cura de aldea cree sorprender la gran figura
que se paseaba en el jardín al fresco de la brisa.
Pero dice la voz: HAGASE LA NIEVE.
Yo creí que la nieve era el cementerio de los ángeles
más ahora sé que el hielo y el fuego
son palabras
              En el diccionario de Dios
el agua es otra palabra
y el viento es como decir Amor
                    y gime.
Esta cordillera es una oración de Dios cuya sintaxis
              solo fue conocida por los misteriosos aymaras
Se paseaba Dios en aquellos días desde las cimas del Hualcalá a la
                                        [Tierra del Fuego
y hablaba con su Hijo sobre la importancia de la tierra.
"Ser hombre es cosa seria", dijo el Señor; es difícil
levantar una cordillera que impresione el corazón de un héroe.
Hagamos los Andes para que puedan producirse
hombres como Tupac Amaru y Simón Bolívar.

GOD CREATES THE ANDES

A crocodile's tear could have been the beginning of the Nile.
In my country, a minor god named Cocijo
gives birth to a river where he urinates.
Chimborazo's snowcapped peak like a gray hair in the air
could have fallen from the temples of God
                                        who moves
his biblical hands like a potter and smooths the summits.
                The Indian invokes the name of Wirakocha
and some old village priest thinks he glimpses the great figure
moving through the garden with a fresh breeze.
But the voice says: LET THERE BE SNOW.
I once thought the snow was the angels' graveyard
but now I know that ice and fire
are words
            in God's dictionary
and water is another word
and wind is like saying Love
                        and it moans.
This cordillera is one of God's prayers. Only
    the mysterious Aymara people understood its syntax.
God walked in those days from the heights of Hualcalá to Tierra del Fuego
and spoke with his Son about the importance of the earth.
"Being a man is a serious matter," said the Lord. "It is difficult
to lift a mountain range that impresses a hero's heart.
Let us make the Andes so they can produce
men like Tupac Amaru and Simón Bolivar.

Estas medidas, estas distancias producirán sueños tan altos como el
[vuelo de un Cóndor.
En esta tierra
es posible que algún día el hombre dialogue conmigo.
Quiero un lugar difícil como la poesía;
quiero, dijo Dios, hablando cosas,
haciendo —con palabras— cosas:

> Volcanes
> Desfiladeros
> Nubes
> Vientos alineados como ejércitos
> Ecuadores

y los ángeles iban detrás escribiendo con sus plumas la creación de los
[Andes.

These measures, these distances will produce dreams as high as a condor's flight.
In this land
perhaps someday humanity will speak with me.
I want a place as difficult as poetry."
Then God said, speaking things, making
things with words, "I want

> volcanoes
> mountain passes
> clouds
> winds lined up like armies
> equators."

And the angels followed with pens made from their feathers,
writing down the creation of the Andes.

HIMNO NACIONAL

(En vísperas de la luz.)

En el límite del alba mi pequeño país toma las aguas tendidas,
las grandes aguas desnudas que descansan—.
"Haré lagunas este día", piensa. Cuenta, de dos en dos, sus árboles,
sus aldeas cubiertas de rocío,
sus territorios que salen despacio noche afuera.
Antes del hombre, aun antes de los gallos
mi dulce país arregla su porción de paisaje:
"Colocaré este azul sobre una nueva mujer",
"Este lugar proyecto para mejores vientos" —va diciendo.
¡A vosotros os antecede, hombres de mi tierra!
Pulsa el alba, otras nostalgias pulsa para buscar el ángel
que circula de sueño a sueño alrededor de nuestros aires.
Mi pequeño país, entre tantos, va historiando sus flores,
la difícil biografía de la golondrina,
fechas de ceibos, de conejos,
historias de hombres rebeldes, otros destinos
en una fuente, en una comarca apenas designada.
Países hay que escogieron calendarios afanosos
para eclipsar las antiguas escrituras.
Llámase Imperio el dolor de unos hombres lejanos.
Se llamará "Inmortal" un nombre arrojado contra el bronce.
Pero he aquí que existe este lugar dispuesto para ser eterno
por la sola palabra que un ángel dicta recorriendo los maitines.
¡Mi pequeño país es habitado por vegetales menos solemnes,
por silencios naturales que van de canto a canto,
entre hombres así, entre montañas asequibles al llanto
y ríos prudentes que transportan con mansedumbre sus estrellas!

NATIONAL ANTHEM

(At Daybreak)

At dawn's frontier my small country lifts the expanse of water,
the great naked water, from its sleep.
"This is the day I will shape lakes," it thinks. It counts its trees, two by two,
then its villages covered with dew,
its territories slowly leaving the night behind.
Before any person, before even the roosters,
my sweet country puts its portion of the landscape in order.
"I will put this blue on a new woman.
I will devise better winds for this place," it says.
People of my country, this land came before you all!
The dawn beats like a heart, the heartbeat of other memories,
searching the skies for the angel that circulates from dream to dream.
My small country, among so many, writes the history of its flowers,
the swallow's difficult biography,
the dates of the ceibo trees and rabbits,
stories of men who rebelled, separate destinies
in a single source, in a single district with barely any borders.
There are countries, eager to eclipse their ancient writings,
that have chosen new calendars.
Let the pain of distant men be called Empire.
They will call any name thrown against bronze "Immortal."
But here is this place, ready to become eternal
at the single word of an angel wandering among the prayers at dawn.
My small country is inhabited by less solemn plants,
by natural silences that move from song to song,
among this kind of people, among mountains that are within reach of a scream
and cautious rivers that gently carry away the stars!

Aquí hemos criado olvidos elementales para ser comunes,
vegetaciones insistentes para cubrir a tiempo nuestras huellas.
Y existe un ángel que repudia nuestras oportunidades
— ¡cierra con insolencia las sórdidas ventanas de los mercaderes!—
y viene urgiendo una palabra más, un canto más
en la pobre aldea que no trasciende,
donde habita ese niño pálido que nosotros desconocimos.
Por eso el alba toma el hilo al sueño desde los pájaros
y va penetrando a todos los que tienen inscrito su silencio.
(Mi pequeño país cristiano se compone de unas pocas primaveras y
[campanarios,
de zenzontles, cortos ferrocarriles y niños marineros.)
"Tenemos este quehacer, esta palabra entre todos", ha dicho,
y así comienza, a punto de los albores, reclamando
a ti, zafiro, llamado último lucero,
al venado, al güís, al chichitote —un pájaro madrugador—
su coro de claridad para alabar la luz.
"Voy recorriendo a tantos, llamando a cuantos tienen ganado su
[silencio":
"A ti, José Muñoz, carpintero de oficio, que sabes hacer mi mesa,
toma este lucero. Sale a guiar su hora. ¡Arréglalo!
Y tú, Martín Zepeda, pues vas de caminante, arrea
estos pájaros. Dales canto o diles ·
lo que sabes del pan y la guitarra.
Y a ti, Pedro Canisal, vaquero, muchacho agreste:
ensilla el horizonte, monta al final la noche, ¡dómala!
Todos sueñen. Todos muestren que están conmigo haciendo
este futuro día, esbelto y sin zozobras.
Busco a Juan, "el Chato", en este barrio de albañiles.
A Gumersindo, jornalero de caminos:
Tengo un ancho espacio que llenar
de Chontales a León, de norte a río, de río a corazón.

Here we have raised the oblivion of the elements like children
so we could have something in common
and persistent plants that will cover our trails in time.

And there is an angel who repudiates our opportunities,
closing with insolence the sordid windows of the merchants,
urging one more word, one more song
in the poor village that will never be known.
We do not recognize the pale child who lives there.
This is why the dawn grasps the thread of dream as high as birds
and penetrates all those who have their silence inscribed.
(My small country of Christians is made of a few springtimes and steeples,
zenzontles, short railroads and child-sailors.)
"We have this task, this word in common," it has said,
and thus it begins exactly at dawn calling
to you, sapphire, morning star,
to the deer, to the birds—the *güis* and the *chichitote*—
its chorus of clarity to praise the light.
I wander among so many, calling to all those who have earned their silence:
you, José Muñoz, carpenter by trade, maker of my table,
take this star. Go out and guide its hour. Fix it!
And you, Martín Zepeda, already on the road, gather
these birds. Give them song or tell them
what you know about bread and guitars.
And you, Pedro Canisal, cowhand, young and rustic:
put your saddle on the horizon, climb the heights of the night and tame it!
Let everyone dream. Let everyone show that they are with me, making
this coming day, slender and without anguish.
I'm looking for snub-nosed Juan, the bricklayer,
and Gumersindo, who does day labor on the roads.
I have a wide space to fill
from Chontales to León, from the north to the river, from the river to the heart.

Esta voz tuya, Gregorio Malespín, cantador de Cuiscoma:
¡levántate!
mira la gente que va conmigo. Ya lo están cantando:
lagos, lagunas, madreselvas,
árboles y campesinos dicen: "Alabado sea el Justo
y Buen Señor que va dando a cada país lo suyo.
Esta noche al nuestro. Este descanso conseguido".
Por tanto,
en alabanza y canto merecido,
árboles y campesinos digan: "Alabado sea el Dueño
de esta posesión. Levantó una noche más y fuese
andando, a cubrir otro lugar de más necesidad".
Porque así agradecemos debidamente este lugar.
Así volvemos a vivir debidamente nuestro lugar.
Mi pequeño país te solicita para la oración y el himno de los que
[vamos a despertar.
Recuerda, hermano, las lomas de Coloja y su césped verde.
Tú, Jacinto Estrada, regocíjate de tu isla, con sus frutales que rondan
[en susurro las abejas.
¡Madre mía, desde el balcón de tu casa bendice mi respiración!
Mientras yo sueño con un canto donde va amontonándose
todo este ritmo patrio de ángeles celestes y verdes palmas,
mecidas, de babor a estribor, por un viento de flautas lentas.

I remember your voice, Gregorio Malespín, singer from Cuiscoma:
Get out of bed!
Look at all the people going with me. They're already singing.
Lakes, ponds, thick jungles,
trees and *campesinos* say, "Blessed be the Just
and Good Lord who makes each country what it is,
who gives us this night and our well-earned rest."
For so much,
trees and *campesinos*
give thanks and praise in song: "Blessed be the Owner
of this possession. He lifted one more night and went on walking
to cover another place that needs it more."
Because this is how we give due thanks for this place,
and return duly to live in our place.
My small country asks you to join the prayer and anthem of those of us who rise from
    sleep.
Remember, brother, the hills of Coloja and its green grass.
You, Jacinto Estrada, rejoice on your island with its orchards alive with bees.
Mother, from the balcony of your house, bless my every breath!
Meanwhile, I dream about a song that builds,
made of this country's rhythms of blue angels and green palm trees
shaken from larboard to starboard by soft flutes of wind.

II

ENCOUNTERS

CANTO TEMPORAL VIII

...Pon una noche espesa, una alfombra de aroma y densa humillación,
desnuda tus pies en un simple murmullo de inocencia,
acércate como el ladrón
sin despertar su muerte, deteniendo la mirada porque su filo es impuro,
y asómate a ese pecho colgado de las cuatro líneas del espacio,
asómate en el ojo de la llave como en el agujero de la estrella,
al ojo de la puerta, al cerrojo de la hermosura y del reposo.
¡Por un hombre se pasa, entre la llaga, al mundo!
El camino es un hilo de púrpura y de agua,
la puerta, en el costado, al corazón nos lleva.
Su nombre lo sabemos.
Lo pronunciara el ángel, el sueño y la paloma,
lo revistió de tacto la castidad de un seno
que nunca fue igualado por línea de mujer.
Y un día en la blasfemia sus letras colocaron
entre la espada y la verdad.
Era el rótulo del reino sobre el dintel de la muerte
porque su palabra es el nombre de los cielos,
porque la cruz es una puerta rota,
un abierto dolor en arco de victoria
para el paso del hombre y la marcha de su canto.

TEMPORAL SONG VIII

Wrap yourself in a thick night, a fragrant blanket of dense humiliation.

Go barefoot with simple words of innocence.

Come closer, like the thief,

but don't wake him from death by staring too long with the blade of unclean eyes.

And look into that chest hanging from the four lines of space.

Look into the keyhole as if you were peering through a hole in a star

so you can see the door's eye and the dead bolt of resting in peace and all that is beautiful.

One man lets us enter the world through his wounds!

The road is a thread of purple water.

The door between two ribs takes us to the heart.

We know his name.

The angel would pronounce it dream and dove.

He was endowed with a sense of touch by an immaculate womb

unequalled in the line of women.

And one blasphemous day, the letters of his name were placed

between sword and truth.

It was the sign of the kingdom above death's doorway

because his word is the name of the heavens,

because the cross is a broken door—

pain opening to form an arch of victory

where humanity passes and marches with its songs.

LA LUCHA CON EL ANGEL

Cuando llegué al límite de la noche
—entre el azul de Abel y el azul de Caín—
a ese límite que te divide
entre tu pasado y tu futuro,
Yo —Jacob— quedé solo.
Y vi un hombre. ¿Era yo o era el otro?
Y este hombre luchó conmigo
hasta que despuntó la aurora.
Luché conmigo y conocí
la fuerza de lo Desconocido.
Luchó contra mí y supe
la resistencia de lo Conocido.
¿Era, acaso, la Fe
empecinada en despejar la Duda?
¿Era Oriente y sus dorados
pabellones contra el cárdeno
Occidente en llamas? ¿Era acaso
la Historia hundiendo su pie en la arena
contra el poder de la Utopía?
¿O era tu Pensamiento
deteniendo tu Sueño, o el Logos
contra Eros? ¡Oh, dime tu nombre
ángel oscuro! dime
quién soy. Dime
Príncipe de los Itzaes,
" ¿Soy éste que soy?",

WRESTLING WITH THE ANGEL

When I reached the limit of the night
—between the blue of Abel and the blue of Cain—
the limit that divides you
into your past and your future,
I, Jacob, remained alone.
And I saw a man. Was it me or was it the other?
And this man wrestled with me
until the break of day.
I wrestled with myself and knew
the force of the Unknown.
He wrestled against me and I learned
the resistance of the Known.
Was it, perhaps, Faith
stubbornly trying to clear away all Doubt?
Was it the Orient with its golden
pavilions against the purple
Occident in flames? Was it perhaps
History sinking its feet in the sand
against the power of Utopia?
Or was it your Thought
holding back your Dream, or Logos
against Eros? Oh, tell me your name,
dark angel! Tell me
who I am. Tell me,
Prince of the Itzaes,
"Am I the one I am?"

porque he mirado atrás —a mi diestra
y he escuchado a mis hermanos
a quienes guían los Presagios
desde que Quetzalcoatl salió de Tula hacia el exilio.
Y he mirado atrás —a mi siniestra
y he escuchado a mis hermanos
a quienes guía la Promesa
desde que Abraham dejó su patria
y emprendió los caminos del éxodo.
Dime tu nombre, tú que luchas conmigo.
¿Tu nombre es Maya o es Griego,
es Nahuatl o Romano? ¿Vienes
del mar o eres aborigen?
Dime tu nombre, te lo ruego.
Más el otro, viendo que no prevalecía
me golpeó el muslo.
Y el Conocido
fue suplantado por el Desconocido.
Y en mi fracaso encontré mi éxito.
Y nunca más pude, triunfante,
recuperar mi paso de triunfador.

Because I have looked behind me, and on my right
I have heard my brothers,
the ones guided by Omens
ever since the time Quetzalcoatl left Tula in exile.
I have looked behind me, and on my left
I have heard my brothers,
the ones guided by the Promise
ever since the time Abraham left his country
and began to walk the roads of exodus.
Tell me your name, you who wrestle with me.
Is your name Maya or is it Greek,
is it Nahuatl or Roman? Do you come
from the sea or are you an aborigine?
Tell me your name, I beg you.
But the other, seeing that he was not prevailing,
struck my thigh.
And the Known
was supplanted by the Unknown.
And in my failure, I met my success.
And, triumphant, I could never
regain my way to victory.

SOBRE EL POETA

Un siglo de ceibo fue iniciado
por un pájaro.
        Bebió
años de lluvias a la noche. Fue creciendo
en materiales vastísimos, de tierra,
de sucias savias y motivos
sólo perdonables en la química. (Un árbol
tiene más culpa, a fondo, que un cadáver;
pero crece su ataúd, se eleva a casa,
a palacio estelar, a fábrica
de febril sudor y apogeo). Ven
a mirar su pabellón de física,
su telar de clorofila —hojas,
frutos, fornicación del polen
y bellotas nupciales: desarrollo
industrial de celulosa, activos
y pasivos, numerales columnas. . .
La estadística muestra
los años de labor. Y los maestros
siempre juiciosos le dedican
su fervor textual y comprensivo.
Pero ¡ved! un árbol
con tanta ley y majestad y células
en números redondos fue construido
para que una rama sostenga
a mediados de abril y mientras canta
        ¡un pájaro!

ABOUT THE POET

A ceibo tree's first century was begun
by a bird.
           It drank
years of night rain. It swelled
with the vast stuff of earth,
unclean sap and forces
that only chemistry pardons. (A tree
is more thoroughly to blame than a corpse;
but its coffin keeps growing, rising to become a house,
a palace of stars, a factory
of feverish sweat and apogee.) Come
see this pavilion of physics,
this loom for weaving chlorophyl—leaves,
fruit, pollen's lust
and the wedlock of acorns: industrial
development of cellulose, active
and passive agents, numbers, columns. . .
The statistics show
all the years of hard work. And those
who are always passing judgment, devote
the energies of their articles to understand it.
But this tree we behold
with all its laws and majesty and cells
in round figures was built
so that on an April day
a branch would bear the weight of a singing
             bird!

III

THE JAGUAR
AND THE MOON

MITOLOGIA DEL JAGUAR

La lluvia, la más antigua creatura
—anterior a las estrellas— dijo:
"Hágase el musgo sensitivo y viviente."
Y se hizo su piel; mas
el rayo, golpeó su pedernal y dijo:
"Agréguese la zarpa." Y fue la uña
con su crueldad envainada en la caricia.

"Tenga —dijo el viento entonces,
silabeando en su ocarina— el ritmo
habitual de la brisa."
                              Y echó a andar
como la armonía, como la medida
que los dioses anticiparon a la danza.
Pero el fuego miró aquello y lo detuvo:
Fue al lugar donde el "sí" y el "no" se dividieron
—donde bifurcó su lengua la serpiente—
y dijo: "Sea su piel de sombra y claridad."

Y fue su reino de muerte, indistinto
y ciego.
               Mas los hombres rieron. "Loca"
llamaron a la opresora dualidad
cuando unió al crimen el Azar.

THE MYTH OF THE JAGUAR

Rain, the first creature,
even older than the stars, said,
"Let there be moss aware of life."
And this was jaguar's skin. But
lightning struck its flint, and said,
"Add sharp claws." And a soft tongue licked
the cruelty sheathed in its paws.

Then the wind, blowing its flute, said,
"I give you the rhythmic
movements of the breeze."
                    And it rose and walked
like harmony, like the measures of music
the gods used before the ritual dances.
But fire saw this and stopped jaguar in its tracks
and went to the place where "yes" and "no" diverge
—where the serpent's tongue forks—
then said, "Let its skin be made of light and shadow."

And jaguar ruled the kingdom of death, undiscerning
and blind.
          But the people laughed at the oppressive
duality, calling it crazy
when it joined accident and crime.

Ya no la Necesidad con su adusta ley
(no la luna devorada por la tierra para nutrir sus hambrientas noches
o el débil alimentando con su sangre la gloria del fuerte),
sino el Misterio regulando el exterminio. La fortuna,
el Sino vendando a la Justicia —" ¡dioses!"—
gritaron los rebeldes— "leeremos en los astros
la oculta norma del Destino".

Y escuchó el relámpago el clamor desde su insomne
palidez. —" ¡Ay del hombre!"— dijo
y encendió en las cuencas
vacías del jaguar
la atroz proximidad de un astro.

It was no longer Need and its grim laws
(nor the hungry nights of the moon-devouring earth
nor the weak feeding the strong's glory with their blood),
but Mystery directing the genocide. Fortune
and Destiny blindfolding Justice. "Gods!"
cried the rebels. "We will read the stars
for the hidden rules of Fate."

And from its pale sleepless height, lightning
heard the uproar and said, "I pity those people."
And in the jaguar's
empty sockets it lit
the terrible closeness of a star.

LAMENTO DE LA DONCELLA
EN LA MUERTE DEL GUERRERO

Desde tiempos antiguos
la lluvia llora.
        Sin embargo,
joven es una lágrima,
joven es el rocío.
    Desde tiempos antiguos
la muerte ronda.
        Sin embargo,
nuevo es tu silencio
y nuevo el dolor mío.

THE MAIDEN'S LAMENT
FOR THE DEAD WARRIOR

Ever since ancient times,
the rain has cried.
        Still,
a tear is always young
and the dew is young.
    Ever since ancient times
death has prowled.
        Still,
your silence is new
and so is my pain.

48

INTERIORIDAD DE DOS ESTRELLAS QUE ARDEN

A Mario Cajina Vega.

Al que combatió por la Libertad
se le dio una estrella, vecina
a la luminosa madre muerta al alumbrar.
— ¿Fue grande tu dolor? —preguntó
el Guerrero.
      —No tanto como el gozo
de dar un nuevo hombre al mundo.
— ¿Y tu herida —dijo ella—
fue honda y torturante?
      —No tanto
como el gozo de dar al hombre un mundo nuevo.
— ¿Y conociste a tu hijo?
      — ¡Nunca!
— ¿Y conociste el fruto de tu lucha?
      —Morí antes.
— ¿Duermes? —preguntó el Guerrero.
—Sueño —respondió la madre.

AT THE HEART OF TWO BURNING STARS

to Mario Cajina-Vega

He who fought for Liberty
was given a star, next to
the luminous mother who died in childbirth.
"How great was your pain?" asked
the Warrior.
      "Not so great as my joy
in giving a new man to the world," she said.
"And did your deep wound
torture you?"
      "Not so much
as my joy in giving man a new world."
"And did you know your son?"
      "Never!"
"And did you know the fruit of your struggle?"
      "I died too soon."

"Do you sleep?" asked the Warrior.
"I dream," replied the mother.

LA CARRERA DEL SOL

"Unseen invisible, but not unknown is fear."
GEORGE BARKER

Para ellos escribo, los obligados
a llevar el sol. La procesión de guerreros
que acompañan el ascenso.
                    "El éxito
es de los fuertes", nos han dicho.
Y marchan en el cortejo del astro
hacia el mediodía con sus lanzas erguidas.

Todos ellos han de morir —los obligados—
para que el Rey ascienda a su cenit.

(Invisible es el miedo, mas no desconocido).

Luego tú contemplas su retorno. La procesión
de mujeres, las abandonadas,
vuelven hacia la noche.

THE COURSE OF THE SUN

"Unseen, invisible, but not unknown is fear."
GEORGE BARKER

I write for them, for those who are forced
to carry the sun. The procession of warriors
accompanies its rising.
"Success
is for the strong," we've been told.
And they march in the star's entourage
with their bristling spears toward noon.

All those forced to march will die
so the King can reach his zenith.

(Fear is invisible, but not unknown.)

Later, you contemplate their return. The procession
of abandoned women
returns toward the night.

"Todo poderío
termina'', nos han dicho.
Y marchan en el cortejo de la tarde
las viudas y las huerfanas arrastrando sus mantos.

Todas ellas han llorado —las abandonadas—
para que el Rey descanse en su lecho.

                       "All power
comes to an end," we've been told.
And widows and orphans march in the evening's
entourage, dragging their shawls.

All these abandoned women have wept
so the King can rest in his bed.

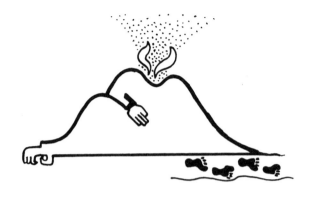

ESCRITO EN UNA PIEDRA DEL CAMINO

CUANDO LA PRIMERA ERUPCION. . . .

¡Lloraremos sobre las huellas de los que huyen de Acahualinca!

Aquí comenzó nuestro éxodo.

Oyeron la gran voz cavernosa del mónstruo
Desde los altos árboles miraron el sucio gigante decapitado,
la espalda rugosa, solamente el rugoso pecho vomitando ira.

Abandonaremos nuestra Patria y nuestra parentela
porque ha dominado nuestra tierra un dios estéril.

Nuestro pueblo miró el gigante sin mente,
oyó el bramido de la fuerza sin rostro.

¡No viviremos bajo el dominio de la ciega potencia!
¡Quebraremos nuestras piedras de moler,

WRITTEN ON A ROADSIDE STONE

DURING THE FIRST ERUPTION

We will cry over the footprints of those who fled from Acahualinca.

Our exodus began here.

They heard the cavernous voice of the monster.
From the high trees they watched the dirty beheaded giant,
the rugged back, only the rugged breast vomiting anger.

We will abandon our country and our kin
because a sterile god has dominated our land.

Our people watched the mindless giant,
they heard the roar of the faceless force.

We will not live under the blind power's domination!
We will break our grinding stones,

nuestras tinajas,
nuestros comales,
para aligerar el paso de los exilados!

Allí quedaron nuestras huellas,
sobre la ceniza.

our earthen jugs,
the plates we cook on,
to lighten the load of the exiled!

Here, our footprints remained
upon the ash.

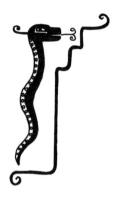

EL DESESPERADO DIBUJA UNA SERPIENTE

Subí a la colina
al salir la luna.

Juró que vendría
por el camino del Sur.

Un gavilán oscuro
levantó entre sus garras
el sendero.

IN DESPAIR HE DRAWS A SERPENT

I climbed the hill
at moonrise.

She swore she would be taking
the road from the South.

A black hawk
carried off the path
in its talons.

LA NOCHE ES UNA MUJER DESCONOCIDA

Preguntó la muchacha al forastero:
— ¿Por qué no pasas? En mi hogar
está encendido el fuego.

Contestó el peregrino: —Soy poeta,
sólo deseo conocer la noche.

Ella, entonces, echó cenizas sobre el fuego
y aproximó en la sombra su voz al forastero:
— ¡Tócame! —dijo—. ¡Conocerás la noche!

NIGHT IS AN UNKNOWN WOMAN

The girl asked the stranger,
"Why don't you come in?
The fire is lit at my place."

The wanderer answered, "I'm a poet,
I only want to know the night."

Then she threw ashes on the fire
and her voice in the shadow drew near the stranger.
"Touch me," she said. "You'll know the night!"

IV

SONGS OF CIFAR

EL NACIMIENTO DE CIFAR

Hay una isla en el playón
pequeña
como la mano de un dios indígena.
Ofrece frutas rojas
a los pájaros
y al náufrago
la dulce sombra de un árbol.
Allí nació Cifar, el navegante
cuando a su madre
se le llegó su fecha, solitaria
remando a Zapatera.
Metió el bote en el remanso
mientras giraban en las aguas
tiburones y sábalos
atraídos por la sangre.

THE BIRTH OF CIFAR

Near the shoals, there's an island
as small
as the hand of a native god.
It offers red fruit
to birds
and a tree's sweet shade
to shipwrecked sailors.
Cifar, the mariner, was born there
when his mother's time
came as she rowed
alone toward Zapatera.
She steered the boat to a still place
while sharks and shad
churned the waters,
lured by blood.

EL ASERRADERO DE LA DANTA

Cargábamos madera.
La sierra circular
en alaridos cortaba
el cedro. El Lago
reverberaba ecos.
El español de barba blanca
llena de aserrín
me hablaba a gritos. Me decía
y alzaba las manos
pero la sierra giraba el sol
cortando el día y el español
gritando más (las venas del cuello hinchadas) "Zifar,
mierda, empuja! ¡ ¿Qué?
cuando salió rompiendo
palos y charriales una danta
negra, torpe, a la estampida,
huyendo de la selva,
tropezando,
cayendo en la sierra
y el ruido
aceitoso de la carne
y el español — ¡Coño!— con la barba
tinta. Detuvo
su dentadura un sol
mojado en sangre
y el animal partido
pateando, agonizante
cuando

THE SAWMILL AND THE TAPIR

One day our cargo was wood.
The buzz saw screamed
through cedar trunks. The Lake
was alive with echoes.
The white-bearded Spaniard
covered with sawdust
was shouting at me. He was saying
something, gesturing with his hands,
but the saw was spinning and the sun
cut through the day and the Spaniard
shouted more, his neck veins about to burst, "Thifar,
you shithead, push! What the . . .?"
Suddenly, breaking through
sticks and brush, a black,
clumsy tapir stampeded
from the jungle,
stumbled,
fell against the saw
and the mushy sound
of flesh
and the Spaniard, "Son of a bitch!", his beard
stained red. A sun
bathed in blood
stopped chewing
and the animal, split open,
kicked the air, near death.
Then

alguien gritó
y volvimos el rostro:
                    Allí
al borde de la selva
el tigre confuso
molestos los ojos
por el sol
miraba.

someone shouted
and we turned:

              there
on the edge of the jungle
the puzzled tiger
squinting in bright
sunlight
was watching.

CALMURA

Rogando al viento
insultando al viento
hijueputeando al viento
o comprando al menesteroso
con la moneda rabiosamente
arrojada por la borda
    — ¡Silba al haragán!
    — ¡Grítale al viento!
    — ¡arréalo!
y silba agudo el marino
y revientan los adjetivos contra el duro
    SOL
que inmoviliza las aguas.

    Pero
    no responde la vela
    flácida
    como el ala de un ave muerta
Arsenio, granuloso
cliente del burdel de Lalita
desesperado de calor
se tira al Lago. Y vemos
    la rápida
aleta del tiburón.

    Al grito de espanto
    como un eco
    aflora del fondo
    en silencio
    la mancha roja.

BECALMED

Begging the wind,
cursing the wind,
no fucking wind!
Or trying to bribe that pauper
with a coin hurled
furiously overboard.
"Let's go, wind!"
"You lazy bum!"
"Giddyup!"
and the sailor whistles sharply
and the adjectives burst against the hard
SUN
that has calmed the waters.

But
the sail remains
limp
like a dead bird's wing.
Arsenio, the pockmarked
customer of Lalita's whorehouse,
can't stand the heat
and dives into the Lake. And we see
the swift
fin of the shark.

Toward the echoing
cry of terror,
the red stain blossoms
in silence
from deep water.

EL GRAN LAGARTO

Esta es la historia
del Gran Lagarto del Lago.
Le decían El Viejo.
Una lama verdosa lo vestía de siglos.

Por ese tiempo en las arenas
del Sontolar crecía un pueblo:
gente huertera inútil a las aguas,
ranas que no se apartaban de la orilla.
Enfrente —en la isla del Armado—
en la caverna
que todavía le dicen "la cueva del Lagarto"
hizo su nido El Viejo. Día a día
se cruzaba las aguas a devorar los cerdos
y ganados. Acabó con ellos
devoró a los perros
y una tarde —a la vista de todos—
se llevó un niño.
                    Una noche
que anclamos en "El Muerto" me contaron
que el pueblo del Sontolar desarmaba sus ranchos
buscando la montaña.
                    Junté a los moradores
los animé con palabras de hombre
y una flota de botes y arponeros
zarpamos al Armado. Las mujeres
rezaban medrosas de rodillas
y tocaban el cielo con sus gritos.

THE GREAT ALLIGATOR

This is the story
of the Great Alligator of the Lake.
It was called The Elder.
It wore the green slime of centuries.

In those days there was a growing village
on the sands of Sontolar. The people
there, growers of vegetables, were no good on the water—
frogs that never strayed from the beach.
Offshore, on Armado Island,
in the cavern
people still call "The Alligator's Cave,"
The Elder made its lair. Day after day
it crossed the waters to devour pigs
and cattle. When it finished them off
it devoured the dogs
and one afternoon, everyone saw it
carry off a little boy.
                    One night
when we were anchored in the boat called "The Dead Man"
I was told that the people from Sontolar were tearing down
their farms and heading for the mountains.
                    I gathered the villagers
and called for action like a man.
Armed with harpoons, our small flotilla
sailed for Armado Island. The women
stayed behind, praying on their knees in fear,
touching the heavens with their cries.

En la boca de la cueva
armé el lazo con el agua a la cintura. Los boteros
golpearon a los perros y a la ceba de su llanto
vimos al fondo removerse el fango
que manchó de sucia antigüedad las aguas.
Luego se alzó una ola, un borbollón
oscuro y vimos
la verdosa pupila, el impasible ojo
y llenos de terror huyeron, los cobardes!
Tiré del lazo
pero, solo, apenas pude esquivar al monstruo
que tumbó mi bote a coletazos.

Si no cayera el perro, si a los gritos
no siguiera a los que huían, a estas horas
no contaría el cuento. A duras penas
pude enderezar el bote
y escaparme.
                    En Zapatera
me esperaban con piedras.
                              Las sombras
me libraron. Y así acabó la historia.
                                    Los cobardes
despoblaron el pueblo.

In the mouth of the cave,
with water up to my waist, I tied the noose.
The boatmen beat the dogs and at the height of their fury
we saw the ooze stir deep in the cave,
clouding the waters with ancient filth.
Then a wave rose, black
and boiling, and we saw
the greenish, stoical eye.
Terrified, the cowards fled!
I hurled the rope
but, alone, it was all I could do to avoid the monster
that tipped my boat with its tail.

If the dog hadn't fallen in, and if the alligator
hadn't followed the cries of those who fled,
I wouldn't be telling this story now. I barely
managed to right the boat
and escape.
      In Zapatera
they were waiting for me with stones.
              The shadows
saved me. And that's the end of the story.
              The cowards
abandoned their village.

EL BARCO NEGRO

Cifar, entre su sueño oyó los gritos
y el ululante caracol en la neblina
del alba. Miró el barco
    —inmóvil—
    fijo entre las olas.
    —Si oyes
    en la oscura
    mitad de la noche
    —en aguas altas—
    gritos que preguntan
    por el puerto:
        dobla el timón
          y huye
Recortado en la espuma
el casco oscuro y carcomido,
(— ¡Marinero!, gritaban—)
las jarcias rotas
meciéndose y las velas
negras y podridas
        (— ¡Marinero!—)
Puesto de pie, Cifar, abrazó el mástil

    —Si la luna
    ilumina sus rostros
    cenizos y barbudos
    Si te dicen

THE BLACK SHIP

Cifar, in his dream, heard the cries
and the howling conch in the fog
at dawn. He watched the ship
    —immobile—
    fixed between waves.
    —If you hear
    in the dark
    midnight
    —in high waters—
    cries that ask
    for the port:
        turn the rudder
          and flee

The dark hull, gnawed away,
outlined in the surf,
(—Sailor!, they cried—)
the broken rigging
rocking and the sails
black and rotten
                (—Sailor!—)
Standing up, Cifar embraced the mast

    If the moon
    illuminates their faces
    ashen and bearded
    If they ask you

—Marinero ¿dónde vamos?
Si te imploran:
— ¡Marinero, enséñanos
el puerto!
dobla el timón
y huye!

Hace tiempo zarparon
Hace siglos navegan en el sueño

Son tus propias preguntas
perdidas en el tiempo.

—Sailor, where are we bound?
If they implore you:
—Sailor, show us the way
to the port!
turn the rudder
and flee!

They set sail a long time ago
They navigated in the dream centuries ago

They are your own questions
lost in time.

LA ISLA DEL ENCANTO

- 1 -

Carmen era una mujer de cabellos rubios
entre mujeres de cabello negro.
A Carmen
las mujeres la señalan
y murmuran
(tiene un gallinero
y en el gallinero un gallo
que sólo canta
cuando la ve desnuda).
La isla de Carmen
era la isla de las canciones.
A la isla de Carmen
van y vienen los botes y las barcas.

- 2 -

En El Anono, la Isla de los Cruces,
un marinero como Eladio
inapetente y pálido
bosteza en el tapesco.
En la Isla de Plátanos
Felipe está encendido
en fiebre: por las noches
se remueve y grita
con negras pesadillas.

THE ENCHANTED ISLAND

-1-

Carmen is a blonde
among dark-haired women.
They point
at Carmen
and whisper
> *(She has a chicken coop*
> *and in the chicken coop a rooster*
> *that crows only*
> *when it sees her naked.)*
Carmen's island
is the island of songs.
Boats and ships come and go
from Carmen's island.

-2-

In the town called El Anono, on the Island of the Crosses,
even a sailor like Eladio
is pale, doesn't feel like eating
and yawns in his hammock.
> On Banana Island
> Felipe burns
> with fever. At night
> he tosses and turns and screams
> in black nightmares.

En la Isla del Menco
nació movido
el hijo de Rosario.
          En Tinaja, Lago abierto,
          cayó en melancolía
          Magdaleno. Apaleó
          a la mujer y a los hijos
          No navega ni come.

- 3 -

Las mujeres de las islas
cruzan de noche las aguas.
De lejos, sus hombres —los jugados
de cegua— ven arder la Isla del Encanto
por sus cuatro costados.

At El Menco
Rosario's son
is born retarded.
>In Tinaja, way out in the Lake,
>Magdaleno is deeply
>depressed. He clubs
>his wife and children,
>doesn't sail, doesn't eat.

-3-

The women of the islands
cross the waters at night.
In the distance, their men (entranced by a
sorceress) watch the Enchanted Island burn
from all four sides.

EL REBELDE

Todavía la aurora
no despierta el corazón
de los pájaros y ya Cifar
tira la red en el agua
oscura. Sabe que es la hora
de la sirena y no teme
el silencio.
Cifar espera
la señal en las lejanas
serranías. Antes del alba
encenderán sus fogatas
los rebeldes.
Les lleva peces
y armas.

THE REBEL

The dawn still
has not awakened the hearts
of birds and already Cifar
hurls his net into dark
water. He knows it is the siren's
hour and does not fear
the silence.
           Cifar awaits
the signal from distant
hills. Before daybreak
the rebels will light
their campfires.
           He is taking them fish
and weapons.

LA LANCHA DE "EL PIRATA"

En lo más oscuro
de la noche
haciendo ruta
de San Carlos
a Granada
    escuchamos cantos
    gritos
       y guitarras.
Al acercarnos
conocieron la vela
— ¡Cifar! ¡Tirá la espía!
Tenemos guaro y mujeres!
. . . Bailaban
       —y sonaban
a golpe de talón
como un tambor
la inmóvil lancha—
pero otros en la borda
desesperados imploraban:
— ¡Cifar! ¡llevanos a Granada!
¡te pagamos, Cifar!
¡tu boca es la medida!

Eran vivanderas,
angustiados pasajeros
comerciantes de los puertos
anclados en la noche
y obligados
a la juerga y al desvelo,

THE PIRATE'S BOAT

In the darkest
of the night
en route
from San Carlos
to Granada
    we heard songs
    shouts
       and guitars.
Getting closer
they recognized our sail
"Cifar! Drop anchor!
We've got booze and women!"
. . .They were dancing
       —the stamping
heels against
the immobile boat
like a drum—
but others on board
desperately implored:
"Cifar, take us to Granada!
We'll pay you, Cifar!
Let your mouth be the measure!"

    They were market women
    anguished passengers
    dockside merchants
    anchored in the night
    and obliged
    to stay awake for the binge.

Compasivo Cifar, tiró la espía
y abordó la lancha de Corea
— ¡Cristóbal! ¡loco
irresponsable!
    gritó entre risas
    mientras ayudaba
    a saltar al barco
    a los tristes viajeros.
    Las guitarras
arreciaron la lluvia de sus sones.
— ¡Cifar! gritaban
— ¡Cifar! dónde está el hombre?!
y manos obsequiosas
le rodeaban de botellas.
    — ¡Sólo un trago
    y nos vamos! dijo con honda
    convicción Cifar.

Pero oyó entonces
una voz que lo llamaba
y vio la loca cabellera
suelta
    de Mirna
bailando
entre el enjambre de estrellas.

. . . Menos mal que el Lago
estaba quieto.
Menos mal que las estrellas
        son
        len-
        tas
para contar el tiempo . .

Compassionate Cifar dropped anchor
and boarded the boat from Korea.
"Cristóbal! Crazy
good for nothing!"
          he shouted amidst laughter
          as he helped
          the sad travelers
          leap to the ship.
     The guitars
made the rain of their sound grow louder.
"Cifar!" they shouted.
"Cifar! Where is he?"
and obsequious hands
surrounded him with bottles.
          "One drink and we'll
          be on our way," said Cifar
          with deep conviction.

But then he heard
a voice calling him
and saw the crazy
loose hair
     of Mirna
dancing
among the swarming stars.

. . .Luckily the Lake
was quiet.
Luckily the stars
               are
               slow
at telling time. . .

LA VENDETTA

Quemaba el sol cuando oyeron resbalar
las quillas de los botes en la arena.
La abuela desde el rancho vio a los hombres
— ¿Qué quieren ellos, Vicenta?
María! ¿Qué quieren los tereseños?
Saltaron a tierra los Conrado
con machetes y hachas
a destrozar la isla. Polidecto
el padre, viejo ya pero fuerte,
sin respetar sus canas, fue el primero.
Le seguían sus hijos y sus yernos
defendiéndose a pedradas de los perros,
talando los frutales
incendiando los ranchos y los siembros.

En el Dientón atarrayaban los Robleros
cuando oyeron en el silencio de las aguas
—que todo ruido acercan—
los gritos y ladridos.
                    Luego vieron
la copa del Malinche desgajarse
y caer sobre los ranchos.
Entonces comprendieron.
Aullando de rabia
doblando casi los remos,
impulsaron los botes. Fuerte es el odio
como el viento. Emiliano,
el más joven (se le salía
el corazón del pecho)
sonó contra la borda el fierro:

THE FEUD

The sun was burning when they heard the keels
of boats slide across the sand.
From the farmhouse, the grandmother saw the men.
"What do they want, Vicenta?
Maria! What do those people from Santa Teresa want?"
The Conrado family leapt onto the beach
with machetes and axes
to destroy the island. Polidecto,
the father, old but still strong
despite his gray hair, came first.
His sons and sons-in-law followed him,
beat back the dogs with stones,
cut down the fruit trees,
and burned the farmhouses and the crops.

The Roblero family was fishing with nets in Dientón
when, over the silence of the waters
(which make all noises seem close),
they heard the shouting and barking.
                    Then they saw
the highest branches of the Malinche tree fall
and crash down on the farmhouses.
Then they understood.
Howling with rage,
almost breaking the paddles,
they surged homeward in their boats. Hate is strong
like the wind. Emiliano,
the youngest, whose heart was bursting
with fury,
banged an iron bar against a gunwale.

— ¡Sobre ellos! Absalón, sobre ellos!
Ya los Conrado remaban a la huida
y en la popa, de pie, gritándole improperios
el canoso viejo alzaba el arma:
—Absalón: la zonta de tu madre
que aliste tu mortaja!
¡la sangre de Griselda
que a la fuerza violaste
te va a morder las venas!
—¿Sangre? ¿De dónde sangre
la puta de tu hija?,
gritó Absalón y los remeros
gimiendo de coraje
echaron la canoa
sobre el bote de Conrado.
Crujieron las maderas
y el machete del viejo
relampagueó en el aire
               como el salto
               de un sábalo
cercenando el cuello de Emiliano.
Gritó el hermano al ver la sangre
salir en borbotones
y con ciega cólera el arpón
hundió en el pecho del anciano.

De la isla vecina los Potosme
—la mujer de Absalón era Potosme—
llegaban de refuerzo.
                    José Maltés
el fogonero del vapor, Felipe
el hombre de la Justa,
Medardo, el tejedor de redes

"After them, Absalón. Let's get 'em!"
The Conrado family was already rowing away
and the white-haired old man was standing in the stern
waving his weapon and hurling insults.
"Absalón! Better have your one-eared mother
get your shroud ready!
You raped Griselda and
now her blood
is going to eat away your veins!"
"Blood? What do you mean, blood? From where?
Your daughter's a whore!" shouted
Absalón. And the paddlers,
seething with anger,
rammed the Conrados' boat
with their canoe.
The wood splintered
and the old man's machete
flashed through the air
        like leaping
        shad
slashing Emiliano's neck.
The brother cried out when he saw
the gushing blood
and with blind rage
sunk his harpoon in the old man's chest.

From the nearby island, the Potosme family
(Absalón's wife was a Potosme)
arrived as reinforcements.
            José Maltés,
the stoker on the steamship, Felipe,
Justa's husband,
Medardo, maker of fishing nets,

y Balbino —todos Conrado—
unos heridos y otros
a filo de machete perecieron.
Murió también el mayor de los Roblero
y Raúl, el marinero de "La Aurora"
y Diego, mi compadre,
que resbaló en la sangre
y caído lo acabaron.
En las islas vecinas
el vocerío se alzaba hasta las nubes
hasta que al fin, ya tarde, como siempre
se apareció el Resguardo
disparando balazos.
Los que pudieron
se tiraron al agua, los restantes
cayeron prisioneros
mientras filas de mujeres
cargaban con los muertos.

Esto contó Cifar en el Juzgado
alegando inocencia. Juró que quiso
detener a gritos la pendencia
pero no hay voz —Señor Juez— que llegue al hombre
cuando habla la sangre!

and Balbino (all from the Conrado family)
were either wounded
or killed by the blades of machetes.
The oldest Roblero died, too,
so did Raúl, skipper of "Dawn,"
and Diego, my children's godfather,
who slipped on the blood
and was finished off after he fell.
On the nearby islands
the shouting reached the clouds
until finally, as usual, too late,
the police appeared,
firing their guns.
Those who could
dove into the water. The others
were arrested
while lines of women
carried away the dead.

This is what Cifar told the Court,
pleading innocent. He swore that he wanted
to shout and break up the brawl.
"But no words, Your Honor, can reach a man
over the voice of blood!"

LA ISLA DE LA MENDIGA

Nechoca-tename —la isla de los gritos— llamaron
   los indios a la pequeña isla de La Zanata
donde moraba, hace años, una mendiga solitaria.
Semejaba una vieja de una edad remota
aunque todos ignorábamos su origen.
Sólo una vez supimos que las hijas de Celso
bajaron a la isla y acercándose a ella le preguntaron:
— ¿Quién y de dónde eres, abuela? ¿Por qué todos los tuyos te aban-
                                                    [donaron?
¿Por qué permaneces lejos de los hombres
y no cruzas las aguas ni te acercas a nuestras islas?
Y las hijas de Celso regresaron contando
que volvió su rostro a ellas
y era una bella mujer de tersa faz y larga cabellera
una hermosa muchacha de ojos dorados nublados por el llanto.
Ninguno creyó la historia de las hijas de Celso.
Nadie se hizo eco de sus palabras
porque los que navegábamos en el comercio de las islas
muchas veces escuchamos los gritos de la mendiga
o vimos a la vieja agitar sus harapos
para pedir, a los que se acercaban, una limosna.
En las noches impenetrables veíamos la fogata sobre el acantilado
iluminando su figura desgreñada y trémula
y los timoneles sabían que la mendiga aullaba de hambre
y apretaban su corazón de pavor desviándose de la ruta
mientras otros, más osados, se acercaban temerosos
y arrojaban con lástima alimentos a la playa.
Una noche de borrasca en que la fogata ardía

THE BEGGARWOMAN'S ISLAND

The Indians called little Zanata Island
Nechoca-tename, the island of the screams,
a place inhabited, years ago, by a lonely beggarwoman.
She seemed like an old woman of some remote age
even though none of us knew where she came from.
Only once did we find out that Celso's daughters
stopped on the island, approached her and asked,
"Who are you and where are you from, grandmother?
Why did your whole family abandon you?
Why do you live so far from everyone?
Why don't you ever cross the waters or come closer to our islands?"
And Celso's daughters returned and told
how she looked at them
and turned out to be a beautiful woman with a smooth face and long hair,
a pretty girl with golden eyes clouded over by sorrow.
No one believed the story told by Celso's daughters.
No one echoed their words
because those of us who navigated among the islands, buying and selling,
often heard the beggarwoman's cries
or saw the old woman wave her tattered clothes
to ask anyone who approached for alms.
Some impenetrable nights we saw her campfire on the cliff
illuminating her dishevelled, shaking figure
and the helmsmen knew that the beggarwoman was howling with hunger
and they clutched their hearts and changed course.
Others, braver, approached with fear
and threw food on the beach out of pity.
One stormy night her campfire was burning,

Cristóbal rompió su lancha contra las piedras de la isla
y salió a tierra desnudo y malherido.
No volvimos nunca a saber de Cristóbal
No volvió la mendiga a agitar sus harapos.
Sólo una vez supimos que las hijas de Celso
bajaron a la isla y acercándose a ella le preguntaron:
— ¿Muchacha, que ha sido de Cristóbal?
¿Es que acaso no sabes que Cristóbal es nuestro hermano?
Y las hijas de Celso regresaron contando
que volvió su rostro a ellas
y era una anciana de faz hundida y desdentada
con los ojos secos y fijos y sin tiempo.

and Cristóbal's boat ran aground on the island's rocks.
He made it to shore, naked and badly cut.
We never heard anything more about Cristóbal.
The beggarwoman stopped waving her tattered clothing.
But later we heard that Celso's daughters
stopped on the island, approached her and asked,
"Listen, young lady, what ever happened to Cristóbal?
Don't you know that he's our brother?"
And Celso's daughters returned and told
how she looked at them
and she was an old, toothless woman with a sunken face
and dry, riveting, timeless eyes.

EL CABALLO AHOGADO

Después de la borrasca
en el oscuro silencio
miraron sobre las aguas
flotando
el caballo muerto.

—Es la crecida, dijeron
los pescadores
       y detuvieron
       la barca.
Las olas
movían sus largas crines.
El ojo, abierto,
fijo su asombro
en el cielo.
       Tendido, la muerte
       lo hacía inmenso.

Sintieron
como un extraño
presagio
       y vieron
una corona
de gaviotas blancas
en el viento.

THE DROWNED HORSE

After the tempest
in the dark silence
they watched the dead horse
floating
upon the waters.

—It's the floods, said
the fishermen
        and they stopped
        their boat.
The waves
moved its long mane.
The eye, open,
fixed its fright
on the sky.
        Stretched out, death
        had made it immense.

They sensed
a strange
omen
    and saw
a crown
of white gulls
in the wind.

NAUFRAGO

Náufrago
      flotaba
—como la esperanza—
entre lo desconocido
y lo infinito.
Buscaba ansioso
la ténue línea
donde el vientre oscuro
se abre a los albores
—No el cielo ni el abismo—
Buscaba
      la lejana orilla
            que las olas esconden
Ver
      la tierra ¡ay!, la seca
la traidora
de donde partí jurando
que no volvería.
Ver
otra vez su cuerpo
de valles y colinas.

SHIPWRECKED

Shipwrecked,
  I floated
like hope
between the unknown
and infinity.
In anguish I sought
the thin line
where the dark womb
opens itself to each new day.
Not the heavens or the abyss,
I was looking
    for the distant shore
    hidden by waves.
To see
  land, yes, the dry
traitor
I left behind, swearing
I would never return.
To see
her body once again
with its valleys and hills.

PESCADOR

Un remo flotante
     sobre las aguas
fué tu solo epitafio.

FISHER

An oar floating
   on the waters
was your only epitaph.

MUJER RECLINADA EN LA PLAYA

No ajena a la melancolía
Casandra me profetiza la gloria
y el dolor, mientras la luna
emana su orfandad.

Todo parece griego. El viejo Lago
y sus hexámetros. Las inéditas
islas y tu hermosa cabeza
—de mármol—
mutilada por la noche.

WOMAN LYING ON THE BEACH

No stranger to despair,
Cassandra tells me her prophecies of glory
and sorrow while the orphan
that she is spills from the moon.

Everything seems Greek. The old Lake
with its hexameters. The islands
yet to be sung and your lovely
marble head
mutilated by the night.

V

FACES IN THE CROWD

PACO MONEJí

AHORA, desde la selva oscura, mi infancia es alta
como la montaña donde los héroes indiferentes
—"vestidos de aire"—
apartan las nubes con desdeñosos gestos de la mano.
Asciendo a la cumbre casi fatigado y reconozco
que era mucho más alto el mundo.
                    Los que transitan
el cosmos no llegarán donde nosotros
colocamos nuestros ojos: ninguna nave
a tres mil pájaros por hora
se acercará siquiera al país secreto
donde un niño lisiado
extraía al silencio
las cosas del misterio.
                    ¡Paco Monejí!
a menudo
un niño perdido
es hallado en el poema! Tus palomas
de barro
        susurraban el secreto
del Katún antiguo. Y las risas
de los individuos
de los invisibles cuando bajaban
de las cándidas galaxias
en una piedrecita blanca. . .
                    Luego
te ladeaste hacia el astro
y salió entre llantos escasos
tu ataúd de cosmonauta.
                    ¡Reposa

PACO MONEJÍ

Now, in the dark wood, my childhood is high
like the mountain where indifferent heroes
"dressed in air"
break up clouds with disdainful sweeps of a hand.
I climb to the summit, nearly exhausted, and realize
that the world was much higher.
                          Those who travel
through the cosmos will never reach the place
fixed in our eyes: no ship
at three thousand birds per hour
will even come close to the secret country
where a crippled boy
drew mysterious things
from silence.
                          Paco Monejí!
Often
a lost child
is found in the poem! Your doves
made of clay
          murmured the secret
of the ancient Katún. And the laughter
of the invisible people when they came down
from pale galaxies
in a little white stone . . .
                          Later
you leaned toward the star
and your cosmonaut's coffin
emerged between sparse tears.
                          Rest in peace

diocesillo!
Aún te miro
—en papel de la China, lejanísimo
como Buda y así de sutil—
elevando tu cometa!
Ah!
Mi paraíso
—mecido por el viento—
pende aún de tu mano
dulce patria
en un hilo!

little god!
    I still see you—
on thin "Chinese" paper, far, far away
like Buddha and just as subtle—
flying your kite!
        Ah!
    My paradise
rocked by wind,
sweet motherland,
        still hangs from your hand
        by a thread!

EL PASTOR O EL PRESENTIMIENTO

(Génesis, 19)

—No lo anima
ni la más leve
brisa— dijo
   Se refería
   a este mar
   muerto
      Y los Sodomitas
   queriendo violar
   a los ángeles
   Y los asesinos
   de Gomorra
   torturando
   a sus prisioneros
   en los sótanos
   —*Por favor*
   hermanos míos
   no hagáis
   semejante maldad
El pastor cerró
su Biblia. Montó
uno a uno a sus hijos
en el viejo Ford
y salió a la noche
   —"Pedro, dijo su mujer,
   es absurdo dejarse guiar
   de presentimientos"
Al subir la cuesta

THE PASTOR OR THE PREMONITION

(Genesis 19)

"There's not the slightest
breeze
to revive it," he said,
    referring
    to this dead
    sea.
        And the Sodomites
    who wished to rape
    angels.
    And the killers
    from Gomorrah
    torturing
    their prisoners
    in dungeons.
    I pray you,
    brethren,
    do not
    so wickedly.
The pastor closed
his Bible. He lifted
his children one by one
into the old Ford
and left that night.
    "Pedro," said his wife.
    "It's ridiculous to let yourself
    be swayed by premonitions."
At the top of the hill

frenó el vehículo
　　Volvieron entonces los ojos
　　los que huían
　　y vieron que salía
　　de la ciudad
　　una humareda
　　de horno

he stopped the car.

> Those who had fled
> looked behind them
> and beheld the smoke
> as of a furnace
> rising
> from the city.

EL HERMANO MAYOR

María, hermana: te cuento
¡fué el acabose! Se vino
al suelo todo
        y quedamos
en la calle con lo puesto.
Los doce hermanos temblando
y mamá
queriéndose hacer brazos
para rodearnos a todos.
A esa hora, ahogándonos
en polvo, oyendo
el estertor del mundo,
a esa hora ¡fíjate!
pienso: —"Papá!" (ya tú conoces
las cosas de mi padre!)
—"Voy a buscarle", dije
y mi pobre madre en gritos
y mis hermanos en llanto,
pero, ¿qué se hace? Cuando
todo cae o cuando
sucumbe el tiempo ¿qué queda
sino buscar al padre?
        ¡Las veces
que le hemos dicho: —"Padre,
la caridad entra por casa"
y él —ya sabes— siempre
en las nubes, siempre

THE ELDER BROTHER

María, my dear sister, I'll tell you what happened.
It was like the end of the world! Everything
came crashing to the ground
                  and we were left
in the street. All we had was what we were wearing.
The twelve brothers and sisters trembling
and mama
wishing she could
put her arms around us all.
At that hour, we were choking
on the dust, listening
to the death rattle of the world.
At that hour, if you can believe it,
I was thinking, "Papa!" (You already know
what my father's like.)
"I'm going to look for him," I said.
And my poor mother screaming
and my brothers and sisters in tears.
But what can you do when
everything crumbles, even
time, except
look for your father?
                  How many times
have we told him, "Father,
charity begins at home."
He always has his head
in the clouds, you know, always

dándole a todos
pero exigiéndonos a nosotros.
Corrí en aquellas calles
negras
cuando de toda la ciudad
se levantaba
el polvo y el lamento.
Me tiraban
piedras las sombras.
Sentí cólera, la sorda
cólera del hijo contra el padre
que lo abandona
                    y lo culpaba
como si fuera el autor
de la tiniebla, el puño
destructor.
                    Estará
—pensaba— ayudándole
a otros. Y así fue.
¿Te acuerdas de Juan
su criado? ¿Te acuerdas
de Juan, aquel que lo dejó
con el trabajo de la huerta
por una prostituta?
                    Con las manos
sangrando
lo encontré en el rescate
de Juan, lo vi
cargarlo,

giving to everyone
but very demanding of us.
I ran through those black
streets
while dust and cries of pain
rose
throughout the city.
Shadows threw
stones at me.
I felt angry, the unspoken
anger of the son against the father
who abandons him.
                        And I blamed him
as if he were the author
of the darkness, the fist
of destruction.
                        Perhaps
(I thought) he's helping
others. And I was right.
Do you remember Juan,
the groundskeeper? Remember
Juan, the one who left him
with all the work in the vegetable garden
and ran off with a prostitute?
                        With his hands
bleeding
I saw him save
Juan,
carry him.

me dirigió sus ojos
llenos de ternura: "Ayúdame!"
dijo. Debí gritarle
¡Padre, padre
¿por qué nos abandonas?
¡Es inútil! ¡Ya lo conoces!
siempre
abandona el rebaño
por una oveja perdida!

He looked at me
with his kind eyes. "Help me!"
he said. I should have cried,
"Father, father
why have you abandoned us?"
It's useless! You know how he is!
He always
abandons the flock
for a lost sheep!

LETANIA DE LOS AVIONES

Madre: sobre el humo de los incendios desciende un avión azul. Es la ayuda del mundo. Ya llega, madre!

Hijo: el avión azul es para los señores que gobiernan.

Madre: sobre la polvareda de los escombros desciende un avión rojo. Es la ayuda del mundo. Ya llega, madre!

Hijo: el avión rojo es para los señores ministros de los señores que gobiernan.

Madre: entre las cenizas que el viento eleva baja un avión amarillo. Es la ayuda del mundo.
Ya llega, madre.

Hijo: el avión amarillo es para los señores militares que guardan a los señores que gobiernan.

Madre: sobre el cielo opaco veo descender un avión verde. Es la ayuda del mundo. Ya llega, madre!

Hijo: el avión verde es para los señores funcionarios de los señores que gobiernan.

Madre: en el cielo limpio veo bajar un avión morado. Es la ayuda del mundo. Ya llega, madre!

Hijo: el avión morado es para los señores partidarios de los señores que gobiernan.

Madre: sobre el cielo del barrio veo bajar la sombra.

¡Duerme, hijo! ¡la ayuda del mundo para el pobre, es la noche!

LITANY OF THE PLANES

Mother: Above the smoke of burning buildings, a blue plane begins its descent. It carries aid from the rest of the world. It's almost here, Mother of God!

Son: The blue plane is for the government officials.

Mother: Above the rubble and clouds of dust, a red plane begins its descent. It carries aid from the rest of the world. It's almost here, Mother of God!

Son: The red plane is for the cabinet members.

Mother: Among the ashes lifted by wind, a yellow plane makes its landing. It carries aid from the rest of the world. It's almost here, Mother of God!

Son: The yellow plane is for the military officers who guard the government officials.

Mother: Against the opaque sky I see a green plane descend. It carries aid from the rest of the world. It's almost here, Mother of God!

Son: The green plane is for the government functionaries.

Mother: In the clear sky I see a brown plane approaching. It carries aid from the rest of the world. It's almost here, Mother of God!

Son: The brown plane is for the people who belong to the government's political party.

Mother: In the skies over our neighborhood, I see the shadow descend.

Go to sleep, my son. For the poor, the aid from the rest of the world is the night!

126

LAMENTO NAHUATL

"Quin oc ca tlamati novollo"
(Hasta ahora lo comprende mi corazón)

Luché
toda la noche
(mira mis manos
hechas sangre!)
Luché
toda la noche
para salir de la tierra
¡Ay!
cuando ya fuera
me creí libre
miré en el muro
la efigie del tirano!

NAHUATL LAMENT

"Quin oc ca tlamati noyollo"
(Finally my heart understands)

I struggled
the whole night.
(Look at my bloody
hands!)
I struggled
the whole night
to dig myself
free from the earth.
Ay!
when I escaped
and thought I was free,
I saw the tyrant's
image on the wall!

VI

TREES AGAINST
THE DYING LIGHT

EL JÍCARO

—En memoria de Pedro Joaquín Chamorro
cuya sangre preñó a Nicaragua de libertad—

Un héroe se rebeló contra los poderes de la Casa Negra.
Un héroe luchó contra los señores de la Casa de los Murciélagos.
Contra los señores de la Casa Oscura
—Quequma-ha—
en cuyo interior sólo se piensan siniestros pensamientos.
Los Mayas lo llamaron "Ahpú", que significa "jefe" o "cabeza"
porque iba adelante. Y era su pie osado el que abría el camino
y logró muchas veces con astucia burlar a los opresores
pero al fin cayó en sus manos.

(¡Oh sombras! ¡He perdido un amigo!
Ríos de pueblo lloran junto a sus restos.
Los viejos agoreros profetizaron un tiempo de desolación.
"Será —dijeron— el tristísimo tiempo
en que sean recogidas las mariposas"
cuando las palabras ya no trasmitan el dorado polen.
Yo imaginé ese tiempo de luz alevosa —un sol frío
y moribundo y las aves de largos graznidos
picoteando el otoño—
pero fue una mañana, un falso brillo
del celeste júbilo, trinos
todavía frescos y entonces
¡la trampa!
ese golpe seco de la pesada loza que atrapa
de pronto
al desprevenido y sonriente héroe.)

—"Seréis destruido, seréis despedazado
y aquí quedará oculta vuestra memoria"
dijeron los señores de la Casa de las Obsidianas
(el cuartel - la Casa de las Armas).
Y decapitaron al libertador.
Y mandaron colocar su cabeza en una estaca
y al punto la estaca se hizo árbol
y se cubrió de hojas y de frutos
y los frutos fueron como cabezas de hombre.

THE CALABASH TREE

In memory of Pedro Joaquín Chamorro,
whose blood made Nicaragua conceive her freedom

A hero rebelled against the powers of the Black House.
A hero struggled against the lords of the House of Bats,
against the lords of the House of Darkness
                              —*Quequma-ha*—
where, inside, there are only sinister thoughts.
The Mayas called him *Ahpú* which means "chief" or "head"
because he led the way. And it was his bold foot that broke new ground.
Often he succeeded in ridiculing the oppressors,
but finally he fell in their hands.

(Shadows! I have lost a friend!
Rivers of people cry beside his remains.
The old fortune-tellers prophesied a time of desolation.
"It will be," they said, "a sad, sad time
in which butterflies will be gathered"
and words will no longer transmit the golden pollen.
I imagined it as a time of treacherous light—
a cold, dying sun and the long caws of birds
pecking at autumn.
But it was a morning, a false shining
of blue joy, the fresh
songs of the birds and then

                              the trap!

the dry blow of the deadfall
that suddenly crushes
the smiling, unaware hero.)

"You will be destroyed, broken to pieces,
and here your hidden memory will remain,"
said the lords of the House of Obsidian
(whose barracks was the House of Weapons).
And they beheaded the liberator.
And they ordered that his head be placed on a sharpened pole,
and suddenly the pole became a tree
covered with leaves and fruit
and the fruit resembled human heads.

Sobre este árbol escribo:
"Crescentia cújete"
"Crescentia trifolia"
"Xicalli" en náhuatl
jícaro sabanero
de hojas como cruces:
fasciculadas, bellas
hojas de un diseño sacrificial,
memorial de mártires
"árbol de las calaveras".

Esta es la planta
que dignifica la tierra de los llanos.
Su fruto es el vaso del indio
Su fruto es el guacal o la jícara
                    —*la copa de sus bebidas*—
que el campesino adorna con pájaros incisos
                    —*porque bebemos el canto*—
Su fruto suena en nuestras fiestas en las maracas y las sonajas
                    —*porque bebemos la música*—
Ya desde antiguo en el dialecto maya de los Chortis
la palabra "Ruch" significaba indistintamente
—como entre nosotros— jícara o cabeza
                    —*porque bebemos pensamientos*—

        Pero los señores de las Tinieblas
                            (los que censuran)
dijeron: "Que nadie se acerque a este árbol".
"Que nadie se atreva a coger de esta fruta".

Y una muchacha de nombre Ixquic supo la historia.
    Una doncella cobró valor y dijo:
—¿Por qué no he de conocer el prodigio de este árbol?
Y saltó sobre la prohibición de los opresores
Y se acercó al árbol.
Se acercó para que el mito nos congregara en su imagen:
porque la mujer es la libertad que incita
y el héroe, la voluntad sin trabas.

On this tree, I write:
Crescentia cújete
Crescentia trifolia
Xicalli in the Nahuatl tongue
the calabash tree
with leaves like crosses:
fasciculated, beautiful
leaves with a sacrificial design,
a memorial to martyrs,
"the tree of skulls."

This is the plant
that gives dignity to the plains.
Its fruit is the Indians' cup.
The *campesinos* call its fruit *el guacal* or *la jícara*
                    —the cup of all we drink
and carve birds on it for decoration
                        —because we drink the song
The fruit rattles in our fiestas as maracas and *sonajas*
                        —because we drink the music
Since ancient times, in the dialect of the Chorti Maya,
the word *Ruch* meant both
"calabash" and "head" (just as it does for us)
                        —because we drink thoughts

    But the lords of Darkness
                    (the censors)
said, "Let no one approach this tree.
Let no one dare pick this fruit."

And a girl whose name was Blood Girl knew this history.
    The maiden bravely asked,
"Why can't I know this tree's miracle?"
And she jumped over the oppressors' words of warning
and approached the tree.
She approached the tree so that the myth
could bring us together in its image:
because the woman is the freedom that provokes action
and the hero is the unhindered will.

—"¡Ah!" —exclamó ella— ¿He de morir o de vivir si corto uno de estos frutos?
Entonces habló el fruto, habló la cabeza que estaba entre las ramas:
—"¿Qué es lo que quieres?"
¿No sabes que estos frutos son las cabezas de los sacrificados?
¿Por ventura los deseas?
Y la doncella contestó: —"Sí los deseo!"
—"Extiende entonces hacia mí tu mano!" —dijo la cabeza—
Y extendió la doncella su mano
Y escupió la calavera sobre su palma
y desapareció al instante la saliva y habló el árbol:
—"En mi saliva te he dado mi descendencia.
Porque la palabra es sangre
y la sangre es otra vez palabra".

Y así comenzó nuestra primera civilización
—Un árbol es su testimonio—
Así comienza, así germina cada vez la aurora
como Ixquic, la doncella
que engendró del aliento del héroe
a Hunahpú e Ixbalanqué
los gemelos inventores del Maíz:
el pan de América, el grano
con que se amasa la comunión de los oprimidos.

Managua. 1978

"Ah!" she exclaimed. "Will I live or die if I pick this fruit?"
Then the fruit spoke, one of the heads among the branches spoke.
"What do you want?
Don't you know that these are the heads of the sacrificed?
Could it be that you want them?"
And the maiden replied, "Yes. I want them!"
"Then you must reach out your right hand!" said the head.
And the maiden reached out her hand.
And the skull spit on her palm.
The saliva disappeared at once and the tree spoke.
"In my saliva, I have given you my ancestry.
Because the word is blood
and blood is once again the word."

And this is how our first civilization began
—A tree bore witness—
This is how the dawn begins and germinates each time
like Blood Girl, the maiden who begat
Hunter and Jaguar Deer
from the hero's courage.
They were the twins who invented Corn—
the bread of America, the grain
that becomes the communion of the oppressed.

EL CACAO

A Juan Aburto

Lo bebían con flores.

En xícara pulida, batido con molinillo hasta levantar espuma.
Era como beber la tierra: un trago
    amargo
    y dulce.
Linneo lo llama "Theobroma": manjar de dioses.
Oviedo, el Cronista, lo encuentra: "precioso y sano"
"E dicen los indios que bebido el cacao en ayunas, no hay víbora
    o serpiente que los pique".
Pero Benzoni, el italiano, lo rechaza: "Más bien parece un brebaje
    para perros que para hombres".
Colón encuentra en su ruta una gran canoa con indios
    transportando cacao.
Los lejanos caciques del Caribe trocaban oro y jade por almendras.
Ana de Austria lleva en sus nupcias a la Corte de Francia la
    fragante bebida.
Y el Doctor Juan de Cárdenas —médico de Virreyes— descubre
    que es bebida contradictoria:
—"Fría, seca, terrestre y
melancólica, como también aérea, blanda, lenitiva y amorosa"
Por eso Madame de Sevigné, moviéndose como una gaviota en su salón
    bebe en la fina taza de porcelana y sentencia:
    "Esta bebida actúa según los deseos de quien la toma".
Y el reverendo Bruce, en Londres, sorbe puritano un trago de chocolate
    y opina:
    —"Es un enardecedor romántico más peligroso que una novela".
No es con vino sino con tiste que brinda el Güegüence.

Ahora somos materia prima.
    Los precios del Cacao en las pizarras de la bolsa de Wall Street.

Y Ezra, en su canto: "Con usura el campesino no
    consume su propio grano".
El cacique don Francisco Nacatime dijo a su hijo:

THE COCOA TREE

To Juan Aburto

They used to drink it with flowers.

In a polished gourd bowl, whipped until was frothy.
It was like drinking the earth:
    a bittersweet
    drink.
Linnaeus calls it *Theobroma:* food of the gods.
Oviedo, the Chronicler of Nicaragua, finds it "precious
    and healthy"
"And the Indians say that if you drink cocoa while fasting
    no snake or serpent will bite you."
But Benzoni, the Italian, rejects it: "It seems like a brew
    better fit for dogs than people."
En route, Columbus discovered a big canoe with Indians
    transporting cocoa.
The distant tribal chiefs of the Caribbean bartered gold and jade
    for the seeds of the cocoa tree.
Anne of Austria carried the fragrant drink in her wedding
                at the French Court.
And Doctor Juan de Cárdenas, the viceroys' physician,
    found the drink contradictory:
"Cold, dry, earthy and
melancholy and also light, bland, soothing and loving."
This is why Madame de Sévigné, moving like a gull in her salon,
    drinks from a fine porcelain cup and pronounces:
      "This drink acts according to the wishes of the person who
      drinks it."
And Reverend Bruce in London takes a puritan sip of chocolate
    and says, "It is an aphrodisiac more dangerous than a novel."
In the *Güegüence* toasts are made with *tiste* not with wine.

Now we are raw material.
    The price of cocoa is listed on Wall Street.

And Ezra, in his canto: "With usury. . . the peasant does not
    eat his own grain."
The tribal chief, don Francisco Nacatime, told his son,

—"¿Quieres ser rico?— Siembra tu palito de cacao".
Pero murió pobre. El árbol
    juega con sus hojas alternas (ovaladas y grandes),
    luego se cubre, como de estrellas, de inflorescencias
    laterales (miles de pequeñas flores rojizas o amarillas).
Y las flores caen y sólo de unas pocas nacen sus "grandes mazorcas
    verdes e alumbradas de roxo"
    con cinco celdas de semillas
    o almendras envueltas en una pulpa jugosa.
Pero es árbol exigente. Y delicado.
    "No vive sino en lugar cálido y umbroso
    y de tocarlo el sol se moriría".
Por eso siembran siempre un árbol a su lado —el Madrecacao,—
    que lo cubre con su sombra gigante como un ángel.
Porque es uno de los árboles del Paraíso
    y requiere —como la libertad— un cultivo laborioso y permanente.
Su nombre viene de "caua", tardarse, y "ca-caua" es tardarse mucho
    porque no es planta silvestre sino un don de Quetzalcóatl a los
    pueblos que escogieron la libertad.
    Antes del Tolteca y del Maya
Cuando Quetzalcóatl no era dios sino hombre entre nosotros
Cuando no se inmolaban hombres sino flores y mariposas a los dioses
Quetzalcóatl nos dijo: "Somos pueblo en camino".
y nos dio el pinol —que se hace del maíz—
y nos dio el tiste —que se hace del cacao y del maíz—:
bebidas para pueblos peregrinos.
Porque esta es tierra de transterrados.
Gentes que sólo llamamos Patria a la libertad.
    Pero vinieron los náhuas.
    Voy cruzando caminos donde los tractores
desentierran ollas funerarias. Allí quedaron sus huesos.
(—*Abuelo: traes a cuestas la memoria de tu pueblo y es pesada como*
                                    un fardo de piedras).
Aquí quedaron sus huellas. Toltecas. Pueblo de artífices.
Fragmentos de una ánfora policromada tan exquisita como una
    urna griega.
(—*Abuelo ¿qué fuego encienden tus pedernales?*). Y leo
en el Libro de los Orígenes, en los anales de los hijos de Tula:
Año 1 Acatl. Año del llanto.
Cayeron sobre nuestras tierras los Olmecas.

"If you want to be rich, plant some cocoa trees."
But he died poor. The tree
plays with its great, oval-shaped, alternate leaves.
Then it is covered with a lateral flowering—
thousands of small reddish or yellow blossoms like stars.
And the flowers fall and only a few give birth to "the great *mazorcas*
of the cocoa tree, green and lit with red"
with five cells of seeds
wrapped in a juicy pulp.
But it is a demanding tree. And delicate.
"It only lives in a warm, shadowy place and it dies if the sun touches it."
This is why they always plant a mother cocoa tree beside it
to cover it with a giant shadow like an angel.
Because it is one of the trees of Paradise
and requires, like freedom, an arduous and permanent cultivation.
Its name comes from *caua* (to take a long time) and *ca-caua*
(to take a very long time)
because it isn't a wild plant, but a gift from Quetzalcoatl
to the people who chose freedom.
Before the Toltecs and the Mayas
when Quetzalcoatl wasn't a god but a man among us,
when flowers and butterflies instead of people were sacrificed to the gods,
Quetzalcoatl told us, "We are a wandering people."
And he gave us a drink called *pinol*, made from corn.
And he gave us *tiste*, a drink made from cocoa and corn.
Drinks for the pilgrims.
Because ours is the land of the uprooted.
We are the people whose only Country is called freedom.
But the Nahuas came.
I cross roads where tractors
unearth burial mounds. This is where their bones remained.
*(Grandfather: you are burdened with the memory of your people
and it is as heavy as a load of stones)*
This is where their footprints remained. Toltecs. Craftsmen.
Fragments of a polychromatic amphora as exquisite as a
Greek urn.
(Grandfather: What fire do your flints light?) And I read
in the Book of Origins, in the annals of the sons of Tula:
Year 1 Acatl. Year of sorrow.
The Olmecs fell upon our lands.

Fuertes yelmos de cuero cubrían sus cabezas,
gruesas corazas del algodón cubrían sus pechos
lluvias de flechas cubrían como un toldo su avance
pelotones con macanas seguían a los flecheros
y a la retaguardia rechonchos enanos con cuchillos de obsidiana
brotaban de la tierra exterminando a los vencidos.
Y ya no habían páginas en nuestros libros para escribir
nuestra historia
sino la lista interminable de nuestros tributos:
Cien gallinas por tribu más cien cargas de cacao
Cien cargas de algodón más cien cargas de plumas
Cien cargas de maíz y 20 piedras de jade
Y cien piezas de loza y 20 piezas de oro.
Y los hijos de Tula comían lagartijas y gusanos.
Y esperaban la noche y unos a otros se decían:
—¿Hemos castrado al sol que ya no alumbra?
Y fueron al templo y ayunaron
y sangraron sus miembros
y con lágrimas y sangre interrogaron a sus dioses
y los dioses les ordenaron partir.

Así emprendieron su éxodo los de la lengua nahua.
—"Encontraréis una Mar dulce al sur
que tiene a la vista una isla de dos volcanes".
Y bajaron los exilados.
Bajaban buscando la tierra prometida.
Y ahí donde llegaban, los pueblos los rechazaban.
—¿Quiénes son éstos? se preguntaban.
—¿Conocemos acaso sus rostros? ¿No llevan
en sus pechos un corazón extranjero?
Y los Mayas los atacaron con sus cuchillos de Zaquitoc.
Y los Cachiqueles los atacaron con sus mazos de Guayacán.
Y los Sutiavas les dieron batalla con sus dardos de Huiscoyol.
Y las guerras fueron produciendo jefes guerreros.
Y los jefes guerreros instituyeron al Gran Jefe.
Y el Gran Jefe no pisaba el suelo - le tendían mantas.
Y la tiranía de los Olmecas les parecía pálida
comparada con la tiranía de Ticomega, el viejo
a quien sucedió Ticomega, el joven
a quien sucedió Ticomega, el nieto

Strong leather helmets covered their heads.
Armor of thick cotton covered their chests.
An arch of falling arrows covered them like an awning as they advanced.
Groups of men with clubs followed the archers.
And in the rear guard, chubby dwarfs with obsidian knives
sprouted from the earth to finish off the defeated.
And there were no longer pages in our books on which to write
    our history,
only an endless list of our tributes:
One hundred hens per tribe plus one hundred loads of cocoa
One hundred loads of cotton plus one hundred loads of feathers
One hundred loads of corn plus twenty jade stones
And one hundred pieces of pottery and twenty pieces of gold.
And the sons of Tula ate lizards and worms.
And they awaited the night and said to each other,
"Have we castrated the sun that no longer shines?"
And they went to the temple and fasted
and bled their members
and with tears and blood they interrogated their gods
and the gods ordered them to leave.

    This is how those who spoke the Nahuatl tongue undertook their exodus.
"You will find a freshwater Sea to the south.
There you will be able to see an island with two volcanoes."
The exiled people went south.
They went south in search of the promised land.
And wherever they came, the people rejected them.
"Who are these people?" they would ask each other.
"Could it be that we know their faces? Don't they carry
    foreign hearts in their chests?"
And the Mayas attacked them with their knives from Zaquitoc.
And the Cakchiquels attacked them with their clubs from Guayacán.
And the Sutiavas gave them battle with their lances from Huiscoyol.
And the wars produced warrior chiefs.
And the warrior chiefs named a Great Chief.
And the Great Chief did not walk on the earth. He was carried in blankets.
And the tyranny of the Olmecs seemed pale
compared to the tyranny of Ticomega, the elder
succeeded by Ticomega, the younger
succeeded by Ticomega, the grandson.

Ahora estamos en la tierra de los lagos
También nosotros fuimos peregrinos. Fuimos
emigrantes y estas tribus llegan cansadas.
Duelen sus lamentos en el corazón de los Chorotegas.
"¡Traemos heridos y enfermos!" —nos lloran. Son mexicanos.
Son toltecas. Son artistas en el barro y en la piedra.
Son maestros en el arte plumario.
Tocadores de ocarina. Orfebres.
Conocedores de los astros.
Y entonces les damos cargadores para que se ayuden.
Les damos nuestros guerreros para que carguen sus cargas.
—"Van de paso", nos dicen. Pero llega la noche
Y entonces con su lengua de pájaros los nahuas imitan al búho.
Y cantalean: "Tetec - Tetec" (cortar, cortar)
Y los otros responden: "Iyollo - iyollo" (corazones, corazones)
Y esta fue la señal y cayeron sobre los cargadores
Y luego que los pasaron a cuchillo cayeron sobre nosotros
Y nos despojaron de lo mejor de nuestras tierras —¡todo el sur del cacao!—
Y apenas fueron dueños de sus árboles
usaron sus semillas como moneda.
No bebió el pueblo ya más el cacao
—Sólo los teytes, los gamonales,
sólo los ricos señores y los jefes guerreros—
"E la gente común no osa ni puede usar para su gana o paladar aquel brebaje
porque no es más que empobrecer adrede
e tragarse la moneda".
Y se vende un conejo por 10 almendras
Y por 2 almendras se adquiere una paloma
Y el valor de un esclavo es 100 almendras.
Y una mujer vende su cuerpo por 10 cacaos.
"Quiero decir que ninguna cosa hay que no se venda".

Cacao:
dólar
     vegetal.

Rivas - Managua. 1978.

Now we are in the land of lakes.
We were also pilgrims. We were
emigrants and these tired tribes came to our land.
We, the Chorotegas, felt sorry for them when they cried,
"Our people are wounded and sick!" They are Mexicans.
They are Toltecs. They are artists who shape clay and stone.
They are masters in the art of plumage.
They play the ocarina. They work with silver and gold.
They know the stars.
And so we help them carry their things.
We give them our warriors to carry their load.
"We will not stay," they tell us. But the night comes
and the Nahuas imitate the owl with their bird-language.
And they whistle: *Tetec-Tetec* (slash, slash)
And the others answer: *Iyollo-Iyollo* (hearts, hearts)
And this was the signal and they fell upon the carriers.
And after finishing them off with knives, they fell upon us.
And they took the best of our lands from us—
all the cocoa trees in the south!
And as soon as they were the owners of these trees
they used the seeds as money.
The people no longer drank cocoa—
only the *teytes*, the land owners,
only the rich lords and the warrior chiefs.
"And the common people do not dare and cannot use that brew
for their gain or their palates
since it would be nothing more than growing poor on purpose
and swallowing their money."
And one can buy a rabbit for 10 seeds from the cocoa tree
And for 2 seeds one can acquire a dove
A slave is worth 100 seeds
And a woman sells her body for 10.
"What I mean is that *anything* can be sold."

Cocoa:
the dollar
          that grows on a tree.

LA CEIBA

Cuando vinieron nuestros progenitores
—"*e viniéronse porque en aquella tierra*
tenían amos, a quien servían,
e los tractaban mal"—
subieron al gran árbol el día en que abre sus frutos
y soplaron sus semillas aéreas para trazar la ruta del éxodo.
Y unas semillas tomaron la ruta de las aves que se nutren de gusanos
y otras las de los pájaros chicos que vuelan en solidaridades y
   se alimentan de granos
y otras tomaron la ruta de los buitres y quebrantahuesos que viven
   de la carroña
      y desde su altura sólo ven la muerte
y otras tomaron la ruta de las águilas y cóndores, la más alta,
la que sólo es cruzada por las mariposas y por los pensamientos de los pensadores.

Este es el árbol de la contradicción
Este es *Vahonché* que cita Landa y "que quiere decir
   palo enhiesto de gran virtud contra los demonios".
Este es el árbol gigante que Gómara vio y quince hombres
   cogidos de las manos no podían abarcarlo.
      Este es el árbol de los Trévedes que cuenta Oviedo más alto que
         la torre de San Román de la ciudad de Toledo.
Y es el que cuenta Núñez de la Vega que tienen los moradores de esta tierra
   en todas las plazas de sus pueblos
y debajo de ellos hacen sus cabildos
y los sahúman con braseros porque tienen por asentado
que de las raíces de la Ceiba les viene su linaje.

   Yo he recordado su sombra antigua recorriendo esta ciudad en ruinas.

En la Calle Candelaria donde estaba mi casa
—hablo de la vieja casa donde yo nací—
ya no queda piedra sobre piedra.
      Y la luna
         ese cuervo blanco
            diciendo ¡Nunca más!
Yo he recordado su antigua sombra aquí donde no hay amor suficiente
para levantar estas piedras.

THE CEIBA TREE

When our progenitors came
*"and they came because in their land
they had to serve masters
who treated them badly"*
they climbed the great tree on the day its fruit split open
and they blew the light seeds into the air to trace the route of their exodus.
And some seeds took the route of birds that feed on worms
and others the routes of little birds that fly together and eat bits of grain
and others took the route of vultures and ospreys that live on carrion
and from their heights see only death
and others took the route of eagles and condors, the highest one,
the one crossed only by butterflies and the thoughts of great thinkers.

This is the tree of contradiction.
This is what Landa calls the *Vahonché*, which means
"upright tree of great virtue against demons."
This is the giant tree that Gómara saw and which fifteen men
holding hands couldn't encircle.
This is the tree from the *Trévedes* that Oviedo says is taller
than the steeple of San Román in Toledo.
And it is the one Nuñez de la Vega mentions seeing in all the main squares
of the villages in this land.
Beneath them the people make their meeting places
and they put hot embers on the trees for a kind of incense
because they believe their ancestors come from the Ceiba's roots.

I remember its ancient shadow moving through this city in ruins.

On Candelaria Street where my house used to be
(I mean the old house where I was born)
not even a pile of stones remains.
And the moon
that white raven
saying, "Nevermore!"
I have remembered its shadow here, where there is not enough love
to lift these stones.

"¡Sal de ellas, pueblo mío!"
Un techo nuevo cubra tus exilios. Un madero
extienda sus ramas.
                    He aquí
lo que estaba dicho en el libro de los profetas de Chumayel:
"Se alzará Yaax-Imixché, la Verde Ceiba, en el centro de la provincia
como señal y memoria del aniquilamiento".

Allí donde nace este Arbol es el centro del mundo.
Lo que tú ves desde su copa es lo que tu corazón anhela.

Este es el árbol que amorosamente sienta tu infancia en sus rodillas.
Con el algodón liviano y sedoso de su fruto tu pueblo fabricó sus almohadas
donde reclina su descanso y elabora sus sueños.

Si suben a este árbol, la serpiente se hace pájaro
y la palabra, canto.

Esta es la Madre Ceiba en cuyo tronco hinchado tu
    pueble veneró la preñez y la fertilidad.
De su madera blanca y fácil de labrar tu pueblo construyó una
    embarcación de una sola pieza
y esa embarcación es su cuna cuando inicia su ruta
    y es su féretro cuando llega a puerto.

De este árbol aprendió el hombre la misericordia y la arquitectura,
la dádiva y el orden.

"Go from them, my people!"
May a new roof cover your exiles. May the beams
spread their branches.
Here
is what was written in the book of the prophets of Chumayel:
"Yaax-Imixché, the Green Ceiba, will rise in the center of the province
as a sign and reminder of the annihilation."

This tree was born in the center of the world.
What you see from its highest branches is what your heart longs for.

This is the tree that lovingly puts your childhood on its knees.
With the light, silky cotton of its fruit, your people made their pillows
where they rest and elaborate their dreams.

Climbing this tree, the serpent becomes bird
and the word, song.

This is the Mother Ceiba in whose swelling trunk your
people honored birth and fertility.
From its white, easily-carved wood, your people built a vessel of a single piece
and that vessel is their cradle when they begin their journey
and their coffin when they reach port.

From this tree, humanity learned mercy and architecture,
order and how to give with grace.

VII

THE SHARK

SEPTIEMBRE: EL TIBURÓN

"Los nicaragüenses llamaron al Gran Lago: "Cocibolca"—Coatl-pol-can, *lugar de la gran sierpe*—Y los españoles, al cristianizar la región, dieron a sus principales puertos los nombres de Santos que vencieron al dragón: San Miguel, San Jorge y La Virgen."

ALEJANDRO DÁVILA BOLAÑOS.

Creyeron los de la lengua mangue que la Noche,
todavía doncella, tropezó cuando transportaba
el ánfora de la luna. Y derramó estas aguas pálidas,
dulces, donde el niño que yo fuí
se asoma por mis ojos
y lee sin cansancio el arcaico himno
de las olas—en el Principio
fué el verso—olas: estrofas
para idiomas inéditos, ritmos
que modelaron, como un caracol
el laberinto del oído.
Un niño vuelve al vientre. Vuelve in-
fante al aire llorado de los peces: aves húmedas
sin canto
y pluma endurecida por una crueldad purísima.
Aquí
ova la muerte desde el principio
su silencio incesante. Aquí
la siniestra aleta—al filo de la luna
rasga la tersa superficie del génesis.

1.

Recuerdo a un viejo pescador
carpintero de ribera, trabajando en la ensenada.
Golpea con el mazo y el cincel sobre la estopa
Sonríe oyendo la risa alegre del niño
que salta entre las olas
Y todo como siempre. "Sobre el dolor
nunca se equivocaron los antiguos maestros":
La brea borboteando en el jarro sobre el brasero.

SEPTEMBER: THE SHARK

"Nicaraguans once called the Great Lake "Cocibolca" (Coatl-pol-can) which means "place of the great serpent." And the Spaniards, after establishing Christianity in the region, gave its principal ports the names of Saints who defeated the dragon: Saint Michael, Saint George and the Virgin."

ALEJANDRO DÁVILA BOLAÑOS

The speakers of the Mangue language believed that Night,
as a maiden, stumbled while carrying
the amphora of the moon. And she spilled these pale,
fresh waters where the child I was
peers from my eyes
and tirelessly reads the archaic hymn
of the waves—in the Beginning
was the poem—waves: stanzas
for unknown languages, rhythms
that shaped the labyrinth
of the ear like a shell.
A child returns to the womb, returns as an in-
fant to air wept by fish: wet birds,
songless,
feathers hardened by cruelty's purest form.
Here
death has laid its incessant silence
from the beginning. Here
the sinister fin, blade of moonlight,
rips the smooth surface of genesis.

1.

I remember an old fisherman,
a carpenter who worked on the cove's shore.
He hammers his chisel on burlap,
smiles at the sound of happy laughter from a child
jumping between the waves.
And everything seems normal. "About suffering
they were never wrong,/The Old Masters":
Pitch bubbling in the pot over hot coals.

El velero y sus disipadas
voces acercándose al puerto. El susurro
del viento. Y el grito. Y la garza
inmóvil en la rama.
¿Dónde diablos se ha metido este muchacho?

2.

. . .Fué en el mes de Septiembre
y "yo, Ismael, formé parte de aquella tripulación".
Bajaron de las islas los pescadores
y rastrearon con lámparas las aguas.
   Aguas antiguas
donde los signos se borran. Aguas
negras, anteriores a la luna, donde pasa
como la culpa, al fondo, la ominosa
sombra.
   ¿No fueron ya vencidos
los gigantes?—murmura el marinero.
¿No cayó bajo el agudo arpón de Enero,
Cuajipal—hijo del fango—el que soporta
sobre su lomo el peso de las islas?
   —Es Escila— dijo el extranjero,
aquella que vió Odiseo y ladra
en las olas negras que baten los Alisios.
Otros decían: —El Kraken!, el engañoso!,
sobre cuyo lomo — creyéndolo isla—
celebraron misa los sacerdotes del Altísimo.
—O Cipactli— dijo el anciano
recordando al temible advenedizo, hijo del mar,
              y levantó su lámpara
iluminando la roca del acantilado
donde una mano india grabó hace siglos
su crónica rupestre:. . .¡la misma historia!.
Cinco círculos dentados y en el centro
el rostro de un niño!
Porque es antiguo
        e inmutable.

The sailing ship and its far-flung
voices as it comes into port. Murmur
of wind. And the scream. And the heron
motionless on the branch.
Where the hell did that kid go?

2.

        . . . It was in the month of September
and "I, Ishmael, was one of that crew."
The fishermen came from the islands
and searched the waters with lanterns.
        Ancient waters
that erase all traces. Black
waters that existed before the moon,
where the ominous shadow passes
in the depths like guilt.
        "Haven't the giants been
defeated?" asked the sailor in a low voice.
"Hasn't Cuajipal, son of mire, who bears islands
on his back, fallen to January's sharp harpoon?"
        "It's Scylla," said the foreigner.
"Odysseus saw her howling
among black waves lifted by the Trade Winds."
Others said, "The Kraken, no one should trust.
On its back that resembled an island,
the high priests celebrated Mass."
"Or Cipactli," said an old man who remembered
how the dreaded son of the sea came from afar.
                        And he lifted his lantern
to illuminate the crags
where an indigenous hand centuries ago engraved
a primitive chronicle: the same story!
Five circles with teeth and in the center
a child's face!
Because it is ancient
                and unchanging.

Sale al mar
y retorna. Atraviesa
los impenetrables líquidos millones de la edad devónica,
—nada en el génesis—
y vuelve
—siempre el mismo— y siempre
oyes esculpido en el viento o en la roca
¡el grito!

3.

En la hermosa oquedad cavada con tus zarpas
—cueva de tus sueños— donde retozas en tus leona-
                    dos atardeceres
viejo dios del agua, aquí, de orilla a orilla
—entre el mástil estéril que alienta la aventura
y el árbol florido en que reposa el orden—
busco al hijo de Septiembre.
Interrogo tu dadivoso piélago, dulce y náutico,
interrogo tu viento terral que levanta de sus cenizas
                        los vocablos abuelos,
interrogo tus vientos alisios locos de fábulas griegas,
remonto, aguas abajo, el río de mi historia
y oigo en el espumoso delta de olas entrecruzadas
                        —¡Bull Shark!—
"¡Tigrones!", claman, alejándose en sus canoas
los nativos. Y el pirata
a gritos desde el botalón: ¡Bull Shark!
                        ¡Bull Shark!
Olisquean desde kilómetros el olor de la brea
y saben que son las naves de la muerte:
los torturados arrojados por la borda,
la carroña de los ahorcados
los acuchillados en los abordajes cuya sangre
llena de aletas vertiginosas el trágico azul.
       John Davis entró con ellos por el río
y cruzó el Lago en bongo y cayó sobre Granada dormida.
Sonaron a rebato los campanarios
pero ya el humo de los incendios

It goes out to sea
and returns. It crosses
millions of impenetrable liquids from the Devonian Age,
swims in genesis,
and returns,
always the same, and always,
sculpted in wind or rock, you can hear
the scream!

3.

   In the beautiful cavity you hollowed with your claws,
cave of your dreams, where you cavort in your lion-
                           yellow afternoons
old water god, here, from shore to shore,
between the sterile mast that calls one to sea
and the flowering tree where order sleeps,
I search for September's child.
I question your generous sea, sweet and nautical,
I question your offshore wind that lifts from its ashes my forefathers' words,
I question your trade winds driven mad by Greek fables,
I follow the river of my history downstream,
And I hear, on the delta where crisscrossing waves churn white,
                               Bull Shark!
"Tigrones!" cried the Indians fleeing
in their canoes. And the pirate
yelling from the ship's boom: Bull Shark!
                    Bull Shark!
From kilometers away the sharks can smell the pitch
of the ships of death drawing near:
those who were tortured dumped overboard,
the carrion of those who were hanged.
The blood of those who were stabbed to death
boarding other vessels fills the tragic blue with dizzying fins.
    John Davis went upriver with the sharks
and crossed the lake in a dugout canoe and fell upon the
              sleeping city of Granada.
The steeple bells sounded the alarm
but smoke from the fires

levantaba coronas de buitres sobre la ciudad destruida.
Así conocimos el inconfundible ruido de los imperios:
el hierro,
el crepitar de ciudades
y un ceniciento aullido de perros.
Porque va
    Y vuelve. "Y es muy suelto en el agua
y carnicero". Como el Olonés,
que cruzó tambien el río
con su cohorte de escualos.
Este es el que partía en dos a los prisioneros de un solo
                                    tajo de espada.
Y gritaba: "¡Mort Dieu! Les espagnols me le payeront!"
La dulce doña Inés de Quirós llevada en rehén por la
                               selva en su traje de novia.
Los trozos de encajes en los espinos guiaron a los indios
y le armaron una emboscada y lo coparon
y lo descuartizaron y lo quemaron y esparcieron al
                              viento sus cenizas.
Pero va
    y vuelve.
500 vacas por una dama cobró Davis
150 por un caballero el ilustrado Dampier
(el terror siempre ha sido negociable)
y escribía con bella letra sobre nuestros árboles
y luego colgaba de sus ramas a los prisioneros.
Pero la dama ya llevaba en su vientre tu semilla
carcharhinus leucas!
y regaló su hijo a una india y el niño
fué corsario, "el hijo de la hembra del tiburón
cuya hambre es amiga de las tempestades".
Este fué Gallardillo el que tomó y quemó otra vez Granada,
el que contaba romances mientras decapitaba prisioneros.
Y así Coxon
Y así Harris
Y así Horacio Nelson (el de Trafalgar)
—el oro de las hebillas de sus zapatos
era robado a la diadema de Nuestra Señora—
Y así Sharp
y Bourmano. Porque va
       y vuelve.

was already lifting crowns of vultures over the ruined city.
This is how we came to know the empire's sounds unlike anything else:
the iron,
the crackling cities
and the ashen howling of dogs.
Because it comes
    and goes. "And this butcher moves
so freely in the water." Like L'Olonnois
who also crossed the river
with his band of sharks.
This is the one who cut prisoners in two
    with a single stroke of his sword.
And he cried, "Mort Dieu! Les espagnols me le payeront!"
The sweet Madam Inés de Quirós was carried off as a
                hostage through the jungle in her wedding dress.
Pieces of it torn by thorns guided the Indians
and they ambushed and captured him,
quartered him, burned him and scattered his ashes in the wind.
But it comes
            and goes.
Davis charged 500 cows for a lady.
The learned Dampier, 150 for a gentleman,
(terror has always been negotiable)
as he wrote with beautiful letters on our trees
and then hung the prisoners from the branches.
But the lady already carried your seed in her womb,
carcharhinus leucas!
She gave away her son to an Indian woman and the child
became a pirate, "the son of the female shark
whose hunger is the friend of storms."
This was Gallardillo, the one who seized and burned Granada again,
the one who recited romances while he decapitated prisoners.
And the same was true of Coxon
And Harris
And Horatio Nelson (the one from Trafalgar)
—the gold in their shoe buckles
was stolen from the diadem of Our Lady—
And Sharp
And Bourmano. Because it comes
                and goes.

En la casona familiar, antes del alba
sonõ el pesado aldabón del zaguán y se oyeron voces
y los criados corrieron con los candiles
y no conocían al sucio Ulises,
al hijo —prisionero de Coxon, el corsario—
diez años esclavo en las islas del Caribe,
musculoso, magro, con las huellas de su desventura.
Y la mano cortada por voluntad propia
para borrar la marca a fuego de su dueño.
"De los tiburones
y de su increíble voracidad—me maravillé con razón"
dice Acosta en su historia.

4.

    Al fondo del país nicaragüense
 en la colina junto al río,
el viejo Capitán Samuel Sherpherd
apaga, como un íntimo crepúsculo, la oxidada
lámpara y entra a la noche
arrastrando los pies. Eterna-
mente iluso sonríe al sueño que retorna:

> *Barcos de altas quillas*
> *luces en los puentes,*
> *roncas voces*
> *de los timoneles, lenguas*
> *escandinavas, germánicas, sajonas,*
> *barcos de Bretaña*
> *con tripulantes hindúes*
> *y el viejo Karol con su humeante pipa*
> *agitando la mano.*

En el cementerio de Greytown yace la gentil Elizabeth
puritana y pálida. Los dos niños
también partieron a los mares antiguos.
¡Oh tierra áspera! flautas nocivas
levantaron como serpientes lianas y enredaderas. Selvas
resucitan de sus tumbas para ahogar
lo que tus manos alzaron. Ciudades
mayas bajo tus ríos. Puertos febriles,

In the family mansion, before dawn,
the sound of the heavy doorknocker at the entrance.
Voices. The servants ran with their oil lamps
and didn't recognize the dirty Ulysses,
the son, Coxon the Pirate's prisoner,
held as a slave for ten years on Caribbean islands,
muscular, lean, bearing signs of his misfortune.
He cut off one of his hands
to rid himself of his owner's brand.
"For good reason I was astounded by the sharks
and their incredible voracity,"
wrote Acosta in his chronicles.

4.

   Down at the bottom of Nicaragua
on the hill next to the river,
old Captain Samuel Sherpherd
puts out the rusty lamp like some inner twilight
and enters the night
dragging his feet. Eternally
deceived, he smiles at the returning dream:
                    High-keeled ships,
                    lights on the bridges,
                    hoarse voices
                    of helmsmen, foreign
                    tongues—Scandinavian,
                    Germanic, Saxon,
                    British ships
                    with Hindu crews
                    and old Karol smoking his pipe
                    and waving.
In the Greytown cemetery lies gentle Elizabeth,
a pale puritan. The two children
also left for the ancient seas.
Oh, harsh land! Noxious flutes
charmed climbing plants like serpents. Jungles
are resurrected from their tombs to drown
what your hands raised. Mayan cities
beneath your rivers. Feverish ports,

dragas, aduanas, mástiles de los activos consulados
asimilados por la vegetación, nidos
de raíces constrictoras, hierbas,
y bajo las hierbas, lápidas:

> Elizabeth Cross
> 1830—1866
> Devorada por el escualo:

En una pequeña caja, como un feto
su mano y su delicada calavera.

5.

Aldebarán no brilla. Ninguna
de las constelaciones del amante,
solo el avispero de las Furias y la cola
del Dragón, crepitan. Has doblado
otra página de tu historia.
Has ganado tu libertad y otra vez la siniestra aleta rasga tus
　　　aguas.
En la penumbra del puerto se acercan remando los
　　　Filibusteros.
La blanca ciudad que tú amas
verá otra vez su aurora abierta a filo de cuchillo.
Madres sustituirán las estrellas con sus ayes
y los fusilados volverán a abrir sus brazos contra el muro
　　　　　　　　　　　　　　　　　de la noche.
Lloro por los hijos de Septiembre.
Isidora, Blanca, Guadalupe,
entran al salón de la casona requisada por el usurpador.
La luz de la ventana ilumina el pálido rostro de Walker.
(Mañana será otro rostro—porque va y vuelve)
Han implorado misericordia por los condenados a muerte.
(La siguen implorando)
Es la misma luz verdosa de las aguas profundas
y no oyen las palabras crueles del extranjero
solo ven sus ojos fríos—*carcharhinus leucas*—la impasible pupila.

dredges, customs houses, masts of active consulates
assimilated by the vegetation, nests
of constricting roots, grasses,
and underneath the grass, tombstones:

> Elizabeth Cross
> 1830 - 1866
> Devoured by the shark

In a tiny box, like a fetus,
her hand and her delicate skull.

5.

Aldebaran isn't shining. None
of the lover's constellations:
only the wasp's nest of the Furies and the tail
of the Dragon crackle. You've turned
another page of your history.
You've earned your freedom and once again
    the sinister fin rips your waters.
Dusk. The Filibusters rowing toward the port.
The white city you love
will see its dawn cut open by knives again.
Mothers will substitute their sighs for the stars.
And the victims of firing squads will open their arms
    against the night's wall yet another time.
I cry for the children of September.
Isidora, Blanca, Guadalupe
enter the salon of the mansion confiscated by the usurper.
Light from the window illuminates Walker's pale face.
(Tomorrow it will be another face—because it comes and goes)
They've begged for mercy for those condemned to death.
(They continue to beg for mercy)
The greenish light is the same as that of deep waters
and they cannot hear the foreigner's cruel words.
They only see his cold eyes—*carcharhinus leucas*—
the impassive center of the eye.

162

¡En vano intentaron reconstruir su paraíso!
¡Volvió la luna
y encontró sus besos en ruinas!

6.

—En el aniversario de la victoria
el corpulento dominador de la isla
me preguntó por el escualo.
—"*Carcharhinus nicaragüensis*"
—Pero no es de aquí—le dije yo—.
Copula en las aguas amargas
y vuelve a las aguas dulces.
Y tocó mi brazo.—"Me interesa
todo lo que me digas".
Pero era él quien hablaba.
Me habló del mar.
"Nadé ocho horas en las aguas solitarias
celebrando mi cumpleaños, dijo (La Soledad del océano
igual a la soledad de las multitudes).
Su perfil arcaico, barbado
como la máscara de oro de Agamenón
flotando en este mediterráneo donde no domina Poseidón
sino Huracán
el dios papagayo con ojo de tormenta.
—¿No es nicaragüense?—preguntó de nuevo.
—Va y vuelve—dije yo. Explota
su poder de adaptación. Depreda
en un reino usurpado.
Y habló de nuevo del mar.
Estaba sentado con el plato sobre las rodillas
desconchando el camarón con dedos expertos.
"Luego se limpió la cabeza del adarce
que en ella había dejado el mar estéril."
Y salió de las olas, fortalecido por la Soledad.
La utopía con su látigo.
—Me apasiona esta tierra—dijo
Y el ojo vivaz, inquisitivo, preguntando por el escualo de las aguas dulces.

They tried to rebuild their paradise in vain!
The moon returned
and found her kisses in ruins!

6.

On the anniversary of the victory
the corpulent tamer of the island
asked me about the shark,
"*Carcharhinus nicaragüensis.*"
"But it's not from here," I told him.
"It mates in the bitter waters of the sea
and returns to fresh water."
And he touched my arm. "I'm interested
in everything you're saying."
But it was *he* who was speaking.
He spoke to me about the sea.
"I swam eight hours in the lonely waters
celebrating my birthday," he said (the ocean's Solitude
is the same as the solitude of the masses).
His archaic profile, bearded,
like Agamemnon's golden mask
floating in this Mediterranean where it isn't Poseidon who rules
but Hurricane,
the parrot god with storms for eyes.
"It's not Nicaraguan?" he asked again.
"It comes and goes," I said. "It exploits
its power to adapt. It plunders
best in a usurped kingdom."
And he spoke again of the sea.
He was sitting with a plate on his knees,
cleaning shrimp with expert fingers.
"He scraped from his head the scurf of brine
from the barren salt sea."
And he emerged from the waves, fortified by the Solitude.
Utopia with its whip.
"This land captivates me," he said.
And his lively, inquisitive eyes asking about the freshwater shark.

Y abajo, acechando desde la profundidad,
la otra mirada,
el implacable ojo
que "domina el funesto lugar bravío y desolado".

7.

Nacimos en el cruce de los caminos. Puente
sobre volcanes. Por aquí pasan los dominadores y los
                                                    dominados.
Los perseguidos y los perseguidores.
Pueblos del Norte llegaron a la puerta de tu casa.
Pueblos del Sur entraron a tu alcoba. Eres el hijo
del éxodo y como tú los peregrinos
árboles cruzan tus selvas. Flores rojas
dejan en tus caminos los Malinches
        —Vienen del Anáhuac
Flores negras dejan en tus montañas los jaguares
manchados por la luna
        —Transportan las leyendas Mayas
y pasan pájaros—emigrantes del zodíaco—
        —algarabía de las lenguas Chibchas
fabricando con picos arquitectos
nidos redondos como los círculos del cosmos.
Aquí se citan las mariposas y las tempestades.
Aquí, como las aves y las lenguas, vienen
los migratorios peces, soñadores
de rutas: ¡peces—misteriosos exilios—especies
que cruzaron de isla en isla tanto silencio
hasta este íntimo mar en el pecho de tu Patria!
Mira el arcaico Gaspar, con su dentada boca de lagarto,
con la armadura de sus escamas impenetrables
—palimpsesto del oscuro Mesozoico—
vino del norte al archivo de tus aguas.
Mira el plateado Sábalo del Sur.
O el inmenso Pez-Sierra
"Con su ferosísima espada llena de colmillos
que yo he visto tan grande

And below, lying in wait in the depths,
the other gaze,
the implacable eye.
"All places else/Inhospitable appear, and desolate..."

7.

We were born at the crossroads. Bridge
over volcanos. Through here, the dominators and the
    dominated pass.
The persecuted and the persecutors.
Peoples from the North came to the door of your house.
Peoples from the South entered the room where you slept.
    You are
the child of the exodus and like you the pilgrim
trees cross your jungles. Red flowers:
the Malinches left them on your roads.
           —They come from Anáhuac
Jaguars stained by the moon leave black flowers
on your mountains.
           —They carry the Mayan myths
And birds pass—emigrants from the zodiac—
           —gibberish from the Chibcha languages
birds who build with their architect-beaks
nests as round as the circles of the cosmos.
Here, butterflies and storms meet each other.
Here, like birds and languages, the migratory
fish gather, dreaming
of passages: fish! mysterious exiles, species
that crossed, island to island, so much silence
until they reached the intimate sea in your Country's chest!
Look at the archaic *Gaspar* with its teeth and mouth like a lizard's,
with the armor of its impenetrable scales—
palimpsest from the dark Mesozoic.
It came from the north to the archive of your waters.
Look at the silver Shad from the South.
Or the immense Sawfish
"with its fierce sword covered with fangs:
I've seen one so big

que un par de bueyes
tiene asaz carga en tal pescado".
Mira en tus aguas los que dominaron por su ferocidad
y los que dominaron por su adaptación
      (Porque ellos fueron como nosotros
      hijos del diálogo e hijos de la protesta)
los que remontan los ríos
de colores que soñarían los ahogados
      —Guapotes, Mogas, Mojarras, Laguneros—
los que descienden de la sal
      —Guabinas, Sardinas, Sabaletes
¡aves húmedas sin canto!
Pero, he aquí! la velocidad y la potencia
—*Carcharhinus leucas*—latín de erres ásperas
para su piel de lija: cinco hileras de dientes,
elástico, incansable en la agresión, y en su ojo
frío
mares de todas las tiranías.
. . . Entonces huyen.
Se hunde en la arena la Machaca,
Se eriza el Bagre. Salta el Sábalo.
Huyen. . .
¡Oh Thánatos!
Entonces tú también alzas tus ojos
y buscas el barco
ebrio de rutas.
"Solo en el muelle desierto, (en esta mañana de Septiembre)
miras hacia la entrada del puerto, miras hacia lo
                       Indefinido".
El navío llega de lejos y rejuvenece tu corazón.
Te citan los horizontes con sus húmedos astros.
Eres tú—¡oh desconocido!—el extranjero
de pie, en la proa,
aproximándote a la aventura y la promesa.
Súbitamente la delgada quilla
corta el tiempo y se abre en dos el mar para tu éxodo.
¿De quién huyes?
      —En tu corazón llevas tu tierra.
      Y a donde vayas transportas tus exilios.

that it could barely be drawn
by a team of oxen."
Look in your waters at those who dominated through ferocity
and at those who dominated by adapting
   (Because they were like us—
   children of dialogue and children of protest)
and at those who come from the rivers:
only the drowned could imagine their colors
    —*Guapotes, Mogas, Mojarras, Laguneros*
and at those who descend from the salt
    —*Guabinas, Sardinas, Sabaletes*
wet birds with no song!
But, behold! speed and power—
carcharhinus leucas—harsh Latin r's
for its sandpaper skin: five rows of teeth,
flexible, tireless in its aggression, and in its cold
eye
the seas of all tyrannies.
. . .Then they flee.
The *Machaca* burrows in the sand.
The *Bagre* bristles. The *Sábalo* leaps.
They flee. . .
Oh, Thanatos!
Then you lift your eyes as well
to seek passage
on a drunken boat.
"Alone on the deserted dock (this September morning)
You look toward the port's entrance, you look toward the
                          Undefined."
The ship arrives from far away and rejuvenates your heart.
The horizons with their wet stars beckon you.
"You're here! Oh, stranger!"—the foreigner
standing on the bow,
taking you closer to adventure and promise.
Suddenly, the thin keel
slices through time and the sea parts for your exodus.
From whom do you flee?
    —In your heart you carry your homeland.
    And wherever you go, you'll take your exiles with you.

¿De quién huyes?
     Y volví el rostro.
Y vi en la estela espumante la ominosa sombra:
"Por cargada de velas que vaya la nao
—dice Oviedo—
le va siempre el tiburón a la par".

Granada, Gran Lago/1983

CODA

"Bajó el muchacho al río para lavarse cuando saltó del agua un gran pez
que quería devorarlo. Tobías gritó, pero el ángel le dijo: "Agarra al pez de
las agallas y tenlo sujeto". Y el muchacho se apoderó del pez y lo arrastró a
tierra. Entonces le dijo el ángel: "Abre el pez, sácale la hiel, el corazón y el
hígado y tira sus entrañas, porque su hiel, su corazón y el hígado te
servirán para remedio."

TOBIAS (6)

From whom do you flee?
  And I looked back.
And I saw in the wake's foam the ominous shadow:
"However many sails the ship unfurls for speed,"
says Oviedo,
"the shark will always swim alongside."

Granada, Great Lake/1983

CODA

"The boy went down to the river to bathe and suddenly a great fish
jumped from the water wanting to devour him. Tobias screamed,
but then the angel told him, 'Grab the fish by the gills and hold it
down.' And the boy controlled the fish and dragged it to land.
Then the angel told him, 'Open the fish, take out the bile, the heart
and liver and throw away the other entrails, because its bile, heart
and liver will be useful to you for cures."

TOBIT 6

EXILIOS

(Dedicado a Stefan Baciu)

Cuando canta el gallo me levanto y veo el amanecer de mi patria
Es hermosa y radiante y mi corazón es un rey que recibe su trono
No. No me iré de mi patria. Aquí moriré.

Pero se pone el sol y vuelvo mis ojos al país de mis sueños
y toda la ceniza del mundo cae sobre su faz
Entonces quisiera ser extranjero
para regresarme a mi patria
Entonces oigo el rumor feliz de las ciudades que no son mías
Oigo la noche llena de exilios
Debo partir, me digo
Y mi sueño es un viaje bajo la tutela de los astros.

Hasta que canta el gallo
y otra vez el amanecer se apodera de mi canto
No. No me iré. Y vuelvo
a levantar el muro con las piedras que cayeron

EXILES

(Dedicated to Stefan Baciu)

When the cock crows I get up and see the sunrise in my country,
lovely and radiant. And my heart is a king receiving his throne.
No. I will not leave the land of my birth. Here, I will die.

But the sun sets and my eyes go back to the country of my dreams
and all the world's ashes drift down to cover its face.
Then I wish I were a foreigner
so I could return to my country.
Then I hear the cheerful murmur of cities not my own.
I hear the night crowded with exiles.
I ought to leave, I tell myself,
and my dream journeys on with stars as its guardians

until the cock crows
and dawn once again takes command of my song.
No. I will not leave. And I go back
to raising the wall with fallen stones.

NOTES

I. ANTHEMS

"Nonantzin"

Netzahualcoyotl (1407-1472): celebrated poet, legislator, and architect. His 40-year rule as Supreme Governor of Tezcoco is recognized as a period of great cultural flowering.

"The Airplane's Old Engine"

The first aerial bombardment of civilian populations took place in Nicaragua in the 1920s when troops from the United States occupied the country and U.S. airplanes were used to attack the "crazy little army" of Augusto C. Sandino.

"Poem of the Foreigners' Moment in Our Jungle"

guás (Micrastur Zemitorquatus): a kind of bird, also called the "alcón collarejo." Its song, according to the campesinos, signals a change in the weather.

heliconias: a plant of the *musáceas,* of which there are more than thirty species in tropical America. In Nicaragua they are called "pacaya" or "platanillo" or "caliguate." The author preferred the general name "heliconia" because it alludes to Mount Helicon where the Greeks received poetic inspiration.

sotocaballos (or "sota caballo") *Pithecolobium Longfolium [H & B] Standl/Mimosacea):* a tree of medium size that grows along rivers and has pink flowers.

ñámbaros (also called "cocobolo") *(Dalbergia Retusa [Hemsl]:* a tree that reaches up to 60 feet in height and has a delicate, fragrant wood that turns a reddish orange color when it is cut.

"God Creates the Andes"

The poem was written by Cuadra during a trip he made with his father to different South American countries in 1934.

Chimborazo: Ecuador's highest peak (20,561 ft.).

Wirakocha: creator-deity worshipped by the pre-Inca inhabitants of Peru, later assimilated into the Incan pantheon.

Aymara: South American Indian group living on the high plateau of the Central Andes.

Tupac Amaru (1740-1781): led Peruvian peasants in an unsuccessful rebellion against Spanish rule. He was captured, forced to watch the execution of his wife and children, and was then mutilated, drawn and quartered and beheaded in Cuzco's main square.

Simón Bolívar (1783-1830): soldier-statesman who freed six Latin

American republics from Spanish rule. He dreamt of a great Hispanic American union under his control.

II. ENCOUNTERS

"Wrestling With the Angel"

Itzaes: a Mexican Indian group prominent in the Yucatán during the centuries just before the Spanish conquest. Chichen-Itzá was their capital.

Quetzalcoatl: literally, "plumed serpent," Quetzalcoatl was worshipped in Central Mexico perhaps as early as the pre-Classical period (before A.D. 300). As the God of life and fertility, wisdom, agricultural processes and the arts, Quetzalcoatl was high in the Aztec pantheon.

A great Toltec king who founded the city of Tula (A.D. 925-950) was a high priest of Quetzalcoatl and called by that name. He had a beard and fair skin. After being forced into exile by the followers of the war god Tezcatlipoca, Quetzalcoatl sailed east and prophesied his return in the year "One Reed" (Ce Acatl). This year coincided with the landing of the Spaniard Hernán Cortés in Mexico. Because Moctezuma, the Aztec king, believed that Cortés was the returned god-king, he facilitated his conquest of Mexico.

Tula or Tollán: the ancient capital of the Toltecs in Mexico from A.D. 900 to 1200, whose architecture, art and religion may have been borrowed by the Aztecs for their culture centered in Tenochtitlan.

Nahuatl: the language of the Aztec and Toltec civilizations of Mexico.

V. FACES IN THE CROWD

"Paco Monejí"

Katún: in the Mayan calendar, a period of 7,200 days. It was part of a series of cycles: uinal (20 days), tun (360 days), Katún (7,200 days), baktun (144,000 days) and alautun (23,040,000,000 days).

"The Pastor or the Premonition," "The Elder Brother," and "Litany of the Planes."

In December, 1972, Managua, Nicaragua, was largely destroyed by an earthquake. It was common knowledge that Nicaraguan strongman Anastasio Somoza pocketed much of the international assistance.

VI. TREES AGAINST THE DYING LIGHT

"The Calabash Tree"

Pedro Joaquín Chamorro: co-publisher (with Pablo Antonio Cuadra) of *La Prensa,* the newspaper that opposed Somoza's dictatorship. He was gunned down on his way to work on January 10, 1978. The Mayans believed that the calabash tree was a monument to the heroic founder of culture, almost always a martyr.

Blood Girl or Ixquic: from the mythic story told in Chapter III of the *Popul-Vuh.*

"The Cocoa Tree"

Linnaeus Carolus Linnaeus (1707-1778): Swedish botanist and explorer.

Oviedo Gonzalo Fernández de Oviedo y Valdes (1478-1557): spent three years in Nicaragua (1527-1530) and was the author of the classic work *Historia general y natural de las Indias* (1535).

Anne of Austria (1601-1666): queen consort of King Louis XIII of France and regent during the opening years of the reign of her son King Louis XIV.

Doctor Juan de Cárdenas: author of *Problemas y secretos maravillosos de las Indias* (1591).

Madame de Sévigné Marie de Rabutin-Chantal, Marquise de Sévigné (1626-1696): outstanding French writer in the epistolary genre.

Güegüence: important example of early Nicaraguan drama written in the middle of the sixteenth century.

tiste: a popular beverage in Nicaragua.

Nahuas: There were two high cultures in Nicaragua before the arrival of the Spaniards. The Nahua, or Nicaragua, immigrated from the north . The Chorotega Indians, who spoke Mangue, were from the south.

"The Ceiba Tree"

Landa Diego de Landa (1524-1579): Bishop of Mérida, Yucatán. He is the author of *Relación de las cosas de Yucatán* (1566), which contains an excellent description of late Maya history and life.

Gómara Francisco López Gómara: author of *Historia general de las Indias* (1552-3).

Chumayel: town in which a surviving book of the *Chilam Balam* was composed. *Chilam Balam* means "secrets of soothsayers." The series of books, written in Spanish characters in the seventeenth and eighteenth centuries, contains knowledge of Mayan custom, myth, prophecy, medical lore, calendrical information and historical chronicles.

VII. THE SHARK

"September: The Shark"

SECTION 1

Mangue language: Manguean languages, a group of extinct Meso-American Indian languages, include Chiapenec, Mangue, Chorotega, and Nicoya.

"About suffering they were never wrong,/The Old Masters" W.H. Auden: "Musée des Beaux Arts."

SECTION 2

"I, Ishmael, was one of that crew." Melville: *Moby Dick.*

John Davis, L'Olonnois (Alias Jean David Nau, Francis L'Ollonois), **Dampier** (Capt. William Dampier, author of *Dampier's New Voyage* [1697]), **Gallardillo, Coxon** (Capt. John Coxon), **Harris** (Capt. Peter Harris), **Sharp** (Capt. Bartholomew Sharp), **Bourmano** (Capt. de Bernanos): all infamous pirates, buccaneers and freebooters who were members of the "Brethren of the Coast" that terrorized coastal cities of the American continent in the second half of the seventeenth century.

"the son of the female shark whose hunger is the friend of storms." Isidore Ducasse, Comte de Lautréamont: *Songs of Maldoror.*

Horatio Nelson (1758-1805): British naval commander in the wars with Revolutionary and Napoleonic France. In 1781, he commanded an English force that hoped to strike a blow at the power of Spain in Nicaragua by capturing their fort at San Juan, taking possession of Lake Nicaragua and occupying the cities of León and Granada. This first attempt of the British to obtain a route for an interoceanic canal failed and Nelson, 23 at the time, narrowly escaped death.

Acosta Joaquín Acosta: author of *Compendio histórico del descubrimiento y colonización de la Nueva Granada en el siglo décimo sexto* (1843).

SECTION 4

Captain Samuel Sherpherd: a name found on a tombstone in Greytown by the poet.

Greytown or San Juan del Norte: principal Nicaraguan port at the mouth of the San Juan River on the Caribbean. This was part of the Transit Route Company owned by Cornelius Vanderbilt at a time when it was faster, safer and more economical to travel between New York and San Francisco via Nicaragua by steamship.

SECTION 5

The Filibusters: William Walker (1824-1860) was an adventurer and filibuster (freebooter) born in Tennessee who was a firm believer in "Manifest Destiny." With a small group of men he eventually took power in Nicaragua and declared himself President in 1856. In an effort to gain the good graces of interests in the southern United States on the eve of the Civil War, Walker legalized slavery in Nicaragua. When he was expelled from Nicaragua, Walker ordered his men to burn Granada to the ground. Walker returned to Central America several years later and was captured and killed in Honduras.

Isidora, Blanca, Guadalupe members of the families of General Corral and the "conspirators" executed with him, including Pablo Antonio Cuadra's uncle, Mateo Mayorga Cuadra. Corral was a distinguished Conservative from Granada who served as William Walker's Minister of War until he was illegally court-martialed for treason and sentenced to death.

SECTION 6

the corpulent tamer of the island: a reference to Cuba's Fidel Castro.

"He scraped from his head the scurf of brine from the barren salt sea." Homer: *The Odyssey.*

"All places else/Inhospitable appear, and desolate..." Milton: *Paradise Lost.*

SECTION 7

Anáhuac: in Nahuatl, "Land by the Water," historical-geographic district which was the heart of Aztec Mexico.

Chibcha: sometimes called Muisca, South American Indians from the area near what is now Bogotá, Colombia. They were the most politically centralized group in South America outside the Incan empire.

"with its fierce sword..." Oviedo: *Historia natural;* see note to "The Cocoa Tree."

"Alone on the deserted dock..." Fernando Pessoa: "Oda Marítima."

BIBLIOGRAPHY OF MAJOR WORKS
BY AND ABOUT PABLO ANTONIO CUADRA

Canciones de pájaro y señora. Written 1929 - 1931 but unpublished in its entirety until it appeared in volume 1 of *Obra poética completa.* San José, Costa Rica: Libro Libre, 1983.

Poemas nicaragüenses. Santiago, Chile: Editorial Nascimento, 1934.

Cuaderno del sur: poemas viajeros. Written 1934 - 35 but unpublished until it appeared in *Revista del Pensamiento Centroamericano* 177 (Oct. -Dec., 1982) pp. 9-24.

Canto temporal. Granada, Nicaragua: Ediciones Cuadernos del Taller San Lucas, 1943.

Libro de horas. Written 1946 - 1954. Published in *Poesía católica del siglo XX.* Madrid: A. Vasallo, 1964.

Poemas con un crepúsculo a cuestas. Written 1949 - 1956. Published in its entirety in *Poesía: Selección 1929 - 1962.* Madrid: Ediciones Cultura Hispánica, 1964.

El jaguar y la luna. Illustrated by the author. Managua: Editorial Artes Gráficas, 1959; rpt. Buenos Aires: Ediciones Carlos Lohlé, 1971.

176

Esos rostros que asoman en la multitud. Managua: Ediciones El Pez y La Serpiente, 1976.

Cantos de Cifar y del mar dulce. Written 1969 - 1979. Managua: Ediciones Academia Nicaragüense de la Lengua, 1979.

Siete árboles contra el atardecer. Caracas: Ediciones de la Presidencia de la República, 1980.

OBRA POÉTICA COMPLETA. 8 volumes. VOL. 1 *Canciones de pájaro y señora* and *Poemas nicaragüenses;* VOL. 2 *Cuaderno del sur, Canto temporal,* and *Libro de horas;* VOL. 3 *Poemas con un crepúsculo a cuestas, Epigramas,* and *El jaguar y la luna;* VOL. 4 *Cantos de Cifar;* VOL. 5 *Esos rostros que asoman en la multitud* and *Homenajes;* VOL. 6 *Siete árboles contra el atardecer* and *El indio y el violín;* VOL. 7 *Tun—la ronda del año—(Poemas para un calendario);* VOL. 8 *Teatro y cuentos.* San José, Costa Rica: Libro Libre, 1983 - 1987.

Works Available in English

The Jaguar and the Moon. Trans. Thomas Merton. Greensboro: Unicorn Press, 1974.

Songs of Cifar and the Sweet Sea. Trans. and Ed. Grace Schulman and Ann McCarthy de Zavala. New York: Columbia University Press, 1979.

Poets of Nicaragua. Sel. and Trans. Steven F. White. Greensboro: Unicorn Press, 1982, pp. 45-63.

Criticism

BOOKS

Balladares, José Emilio. *Pablo Antonio Cuadra: La palabra y el tiempo (secuencia y estructura en su creación poetica).* San José, Costa Rica: Libro Libre, 1986.

Guardia de Alfaro, Gloria. *Estudio sobre el pensamiento poético de Pablo Antonio Cuadra.* Madrid: Editorial Gredos, 1971.

Felz, Jean-Louis. *L'Oeuvre de Pablo Antonio Cuadra: recherche d'une culture nicaraguayenne.* (2 volumes) Paris: Université de la Sorbonne Nouvelle, Études Latino-américaines, 1981.

ARTICLES

Revista del Pensamiento Centroamericano. 177 (Oct. - Dec., 1982). Entire issue on Pablo Antonio Cuadra.

Interview

In *Culture & Politics in Nicaragua: Testimonies of Poets and Writers.* Steven White, Ed. New York: Lumen Books, 1986, pp. 14-36.

BIOGRAPHICAL NOTES

STEVEN F. WHITE was born in Abington, Pennsylvania in 1955 and was raised in Glencoe, Illinois. He was educated at Williams College and the University of Oregon. He has traveled extensively throughout Latin America. In 1983 he received a Fulbright grant to translate poetry in Chile. He lives with his wife and son in Canton, New York, where he has taught at St. Lawrence University since September, 1987.

Unicorn Press has published his first two collections of poetry, *Burning the Old Year* and *For the Unborn,* as well as the bilingual anthologies *Poets of Nicaragua: 1918 - 1979* and *Poets of Chile: 1965 - 1985.* Lumen Books recently brought out *Culture & Politics in Nicaragua.* His new translation (with Greg Simon) of Federico García Lorca's *Poeta en Nueva York* has just been published by Farrar, Straus & Giroux.

JORGE EDUARDO ARELLANO was born in Granada, Nicaragua in 1946 and studied literature in Madrid, specializing in Hispanic Philology, Documentation and Archives. Recently he has lectured at Princeton and at Georgetown University. He is the author of many fundamental works on Nicaraguan literature, art and history, including *Panorama de la literatura nicaragüense* and *Antología general de la poesía nicaragüense.* In 1983 he published his most recent volume of poems, *La entrega de los dones.* He currently resides in Managua with his wife and four children.